To/

Lewis
Merry Christmas
1999
Dannie, Heather,
Andrew, Ewan
and Duncan
xxx

SOCCER SUPERSTARS
★ 1999-2000 ★

‖ •PARRAGON• ‖

SOCCER SUPERSTARS
★ 1999-2000 ★

Produced by International Publishing Associates

Words: Paul Fry
Design: Lance Bellers
Image Quality and Scanning: John Symonds

First published in 1999 by Parragon

Parragon
Queen Street House
4 Queen Street
Bath BA1 1HE
United Kingdom

ISBN: 0 75252 962 5

CONTENTS

JORG ALBERTZ

STATS

Age	28	
Born	29 January 1971, Monchengladbach, Germany	
Size	6'2", 13st 5lbs	
Position	Midfielder	

Club	League Apps	League Goals
SV Hamburg	34	9
Rangers	77	24

German International

Transfers Involving British Clubs

Hamburg to Rangers, July 1996, £4m

Honours

Scottish League 1997, 1999; Scottish Cup 1999, runner-up 1998; Scottish League Cup 1997, 1999

Memorable 'Gers Match

In Dick Advocaat's first match in charge in July 1998, Rangers trailed Irish side Shelbourne 3-0 in a UEFA Cup tie when they were awarded a penalty just before the hour. With a goal vital to steady the nerves, Jorg smashed the spot kick home and went on to grab the last goal, also from the spot, in a remarkable 5-3 comeback win.

DID YOU KNOW

Jorg can strike the ball at speeds close to 100mph, giving him the most powerful shot in the Scottish Premier League

Albertz has scored almost 50 goals for Rangers but may have to move to another League to kick-start an international career

JORG ALBERTZ is the German who thinks he's a Scot. The man nicknamed the Hammer says he didn't think the Rangers dressing-room had enough players with blue in their veins, so me appointed himself an honourary Scot as the 'Gers reclaimed the Scottish title from arch-rivals Celtic last term.

'When we got badly beaten by Celtic, it really got to me. I consider myself to be half Scottish now and I take that role on before big games to remind the other lads of exactly what this is all about,' he says.

He wears his heart on his sleeve and took great delight in scoring as Rangers won at Celtic Park to seal their tenth championship in 11 years.

The former Hamburg midfielder thought his days at Ibrox might be numbered with the arrival of Neil McCann. But Albertz, whose goals record from midfield is formidable, has more than held his own with a series of spirited performances.

The arrival of fellow German, goalkeeper Steffan Klos, gave Albertz the chance to practice his mother language – but he declines in order to help Klos come to terms with life in Scotland.

It has been Albertz's willingness to settle that has seen him become such a big favourite with the Gers fans. But he takes nothing for granted, recalling the time at Hamburg when boss Dick Advocaat, then in charge of the German side, dropped him for a UEFA Cup tie. 'There was no row,' he says. 'I was dropped because I wasn't playing well, so I just trained harder and fought my way back into the side.'

Aside from winning the title, one of the highlights last term for Albertz was his first Rangers hat-trick – and the first of his career – in a 6-1 win over Dundee, their biggest in the Premiership.

He also played provider to devastating effect, setting up some of the other goals. McCann, one of the grateful recipients, said: 'Jorg is a brilliant reader of the game and likes to make the killer pass which means you have to get inside the full-back.'

Albertz has scored almost 50 goals in two-and-a-half years at Ibrox, many from the penalty spot, or long range. But he craves a return to the German international side and fears he may have to move in order to do it.

Tottenham's George Graham was said to have been tracking him, and there would be no shortage of offers from the Bundesliga. But Rangers fans would be sad to see their adopted Scot leave Glasgow.

DARREN ANDERTON
TOTTENHAM HOTSPUR

DID YOU KNOW

Darren wears contact lenses, and missed several minutes of the 1998 England v Argentina World Cup match after one was knocked out!

Anderton limbers up for a bit of energetic training

GEORGE GRAHAM got his first warning of Darren Anderton's abilities in June 1992 when his old pal Terry Venables called him.

'I have just signed one of the best athletes in the country. He runs for fun and he can play,' said Venables, then the Spurs boss, who was trumpeting his £1.75m purchase from Portsmouth.

But it is only now, having shrugged off his 'sicknote' tag for always being injured, that Anderton has finally begun to earn his spurs. And it is Graham, once of Arsenal of course, who has benefited!

'There was a time when I would look up at the clock and there were 20 minutes to go. I was wishing the time away because I felt really tired,' admits England wide man Anderton. 'Now, if there are only a few minutes left and we are doing well, I am disappointed. I feel the fittest I've ever been.'

Injuries have cost thoroughbred Anderton countless appearances for club and country – but left him hungry for success. Though he thought his chances of a Wembley appearance had gone until Graham's arrival at White Hart Lane. After the hard-fought Worthington Cup semi-final win against Wimbledon, he said: 'The feeling at the final whistle was one of the greatest in my career.

'The only thing that was better was when I scored against Colombia in the World Cup. If I'm honest, it was probably the worst game I've ever played in. It was horrible, on a terrible, dreadful pitch – but when we'd won, it didn't matter.'

Anderton had suffered semi-final agony with Portsmouth, Spurs and England and said: 'I was beginning to feel I was jinxed. 'Everybody knows about the semi-finals I've lost as a professional, but I also lost in the FA Youth Cup semis with Pompey. When it keeps on happening it makes you think you'll never win one.'

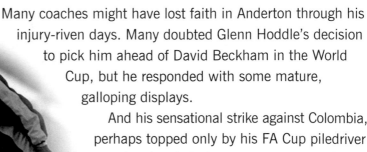

Many coaches might have lost faith in Anderton through his injury-riven days. Many doubted Glenn Hoddle's decision to pick him ahead of David Beckham in the World Cup, but he responded with some mature, galloping displays.

And his sensational strike against Colombia, perhaps topped only by his FA Cup piledriver against Leeds last season, was more than his just reward for years of pain.

Now, with long-term injuries behind him and his semi-final duck broken, it seems only happy days are ahead for this talented athlete.

NICOLAS ANELKA

ARSENAL

STATS

Age	20
Born	24 March 1979, Versailles, France
Size	6'0", 12st 3lbs
Position	Striker

Club	League Apps	League Goals
Paris St Germain	10	1
Arsenal	65	23

French International

Transfers Involving British Clubs

Paris SG to Arsenal, March 1997, £500,000 plus more depending on appearances

Honours

Premiership 1998; FA Cup 1998

Memorable Gunners' Match

The 1998 FA Cup Final saw Nicolas finish Newcastle off, with a superbly taken second goal as Arsenal sealed the double with a convincing 2-0 win.

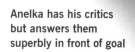

DID YOU KNOW

Nicolas scored the goals for France that beat England 2-0 at Wembley in February 1999 – and had another goal ruled out incorrectly for offside.

Anelka has his critics but answers them superbly in front of goal

MUCH AS Arsene Wenger was worshipped by the Highbury faithful after delivering a Premiership and FA Cup Double, many fans doubted his wisdom in having so much faith in a 19-year-old homesick French striker.

What's more, that faith was placed in Nicolas Anelka at the expense of Highbury legend Ian Wright.

But those same doubters have been left to eat their words. The more so following his wonderful double strike for the World champions in a 2-0 win against England – the first for France at Wembley.

'I got goosebumps watching him,' said Raymond Kopa, star of the 1958 World Cup for France. 'For too long we have lacked a quality striker, Anelka completes the package.'

Still only 20, the powerful, pacy Anelka was 'stolen' from Paris St Germain by Wenger, who exploited a loophole in the French transfer system. He might have become the central figure in the sort of legal battle that made Jean-Marc Bosman famous, until PSG relented and Arsenal picked up the player for a small compensation fee.

Anelka's success has seen still more young French talent leave the country, and prompted moves to make it easier for French clubs to hold on to their young stars.

For Arsenal fans, though, there has been the persistent worry that Anelka, who has never truly settled in England, might leave.

The signals have been confusing. Anelka says he misses his friends, finds the English ways of going out to pubs 'boring' – and yet says he will see out his new four-year deal at Highbury, disappointing Juventus, Real Madrid and others.

Prone to sulking, he's had run-ins with Dutch team-mates Marc Overmars and Dennis Bergkamp for supposedly not passing too him.

But Anelka has also answered any criticism where it matters – in front of goal. A nervous finisher at first, he is now finding the net with a growing percentage of his attempts.

It was Anelka's galloping goal that secured the FA Cup as the Gunners tied up the Double, and he was among last season's leading Premiership marksmen.

'He is still very young,' says the ever-defensive Wenger. 'He is playing on a big stage, away from home. But he is maturing very fast, scoring crucial goals at crucial moments.'

DAVID BECKHAM

MANCHESTER UNITED

STATS

Age	24	
Born	2 May 1975, Leytonstone, London	
Size	6'0", 11st 12lbs	
Position	Midfielder	

Club	League Apps	League Goals
Preston (loan)	5	2
Manchester United	110	29

England International

22 appearances, 1 goal

Transfers

None, signed from trainee

Honours

European Cup 1999; Premiership 1996, 1997, 1999; FA Cup 1996, 1999; Charity Shield 1996, 1997; FA Youth Cup 1992; PFA Young Player Of The Year 1997; Match Of The Day Goal Of The Season 1997

Memorable United Match

On the first day of the 1996-97 season, Manchester United played Wimbledon at Selhurst Park. With his team winning 2-0 in the last minute, the ball came to David on the right touchline, just inside his half. He rolled the ball forward, saw Wimbledon keeper Neil Sullivan just off his line, and struck a powerful lob from 60 yards or so which the desparing Sullivamn couldn't keep out. A stunning goal.

DID YOU KNOW

David is one of three current United players to be Young Player Of The Year – Ryan Giggs won the award twice, and Andy Cole won it when he was at Newcastle.

WHAT A DIFFERENCE a few months can make! David Beckham went from Public Enemy No. 1 to hero last season – and he had Argentinian hatchet man Diego Simeone to thank for it...

The Inter hard-man star was involved in that infamous World Cup incident in which Beckham was sent off, and blamed by many for his team's early exit from the competition in France. Hate mail, abuse at grounds – Beckham was an easy target for the boo boys when he returned home.

But what goes around sometimes comes around, and for Beckham, the day he finally became a man can be said to be that memorable evening at Old Trafford in March when Manchester United beat Simeone's Inter Milan 2-0, with Beckham the architect of a fantastic Reds performance, and even better result, and two goals for the electric Dwight Yorke.

At the end, Beckham shook Simeone's hand and swapped shirts – probably the most outstanding piece of sportsmanship seen on a British football field for years. The feud was over, Beckham finally put his demons to rest and became the all-round football talent and person Sir Bobby Charlton knew he would become when the young east Londoner graced one of his soccer schools.

Fatherhood, too, has played a part in the maturing of Beckham. Wife Victoria 'Posh Spice' provided him with a son, Brooklyn, whose name David proudly had stitched onto his football boots. His pop star wife has been there for him through the most trying of times.

If Eric Cantona was the definitive United No.7, the mercurial Frenchman now has a worthy challenger in Beckham.

Beckham is maturing into a world class player

'David has grown up fast,' says manager Alex Ferguson. 'Becoming a father has been a big help. But the World Cup thing is now ancient history for him. He learnt from that and you have to admire his character in putting it all behind him.'

At 24, Beckham is still short of his prime and as hungry as ever for success with both club and country.

He'll probably never completely lose his streak of rashness, but his new-found responsibilities in his private life have spilled into his professional life. And that is a massive plus for Manchester United.

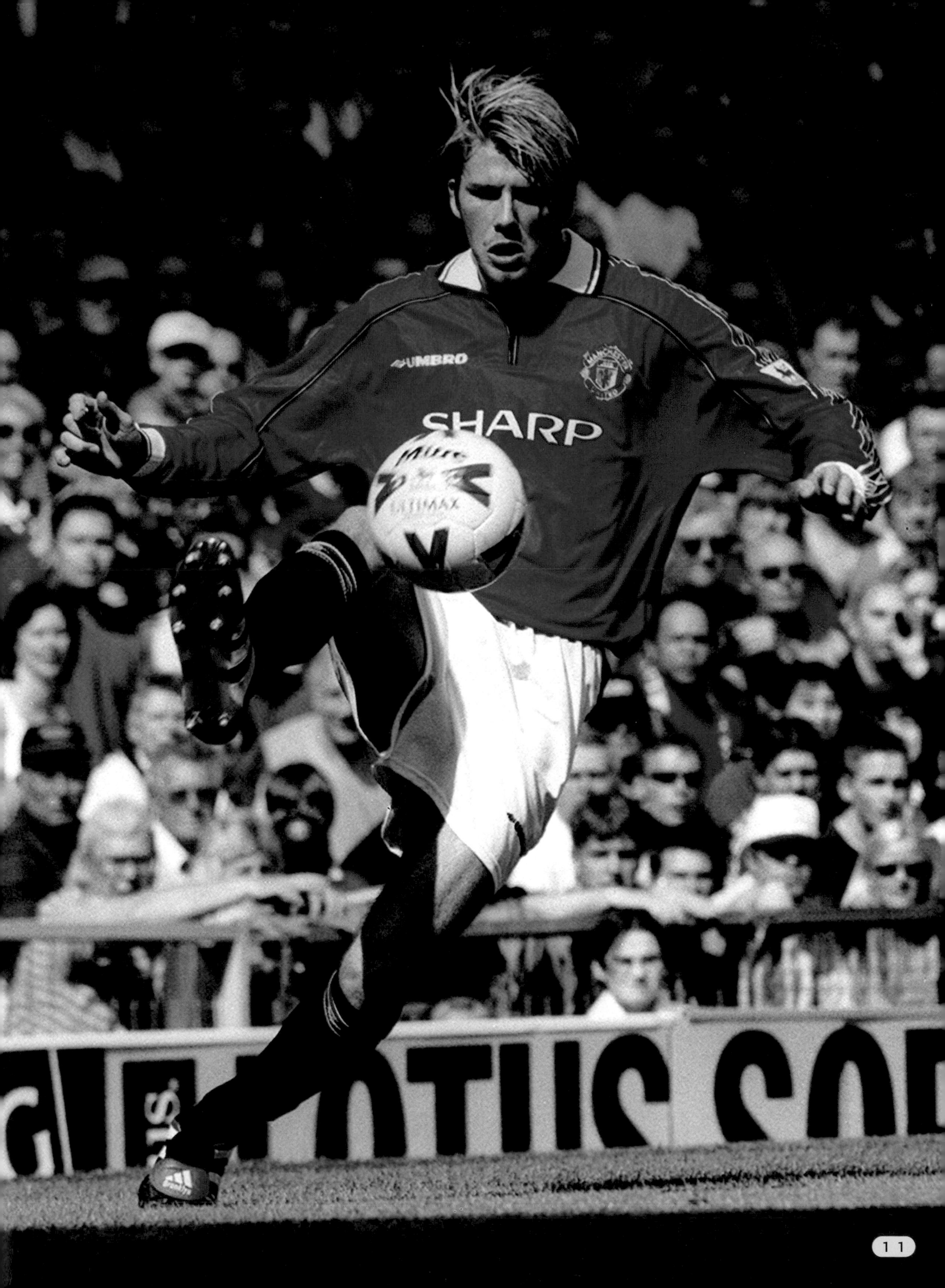
UMBRO
SHARP

DENNIS BERGKAMP
ARSENAL

STATS

Age	30	
Born	18 May 1969	
	Amsterdam, Holland	
Size	6'0", 12st 5lbs	
Position	Striker	

Club	League apps	League goals
Ajax	185	103
Inter Milan	52	11
Arsenal	119	51

Dutch International

68 appearance, 36 goals

Transfers

Ajax to Inter Milan, July 1993 £8m

Inter Milan to Arsenal, July 1995 £7m

Honours

Dutch Championship 1990; Dutch Cup 1987, 1993; European Cup Winners' Cup 1987; UEFA Cup 1992 (Ajax), 1994 (Inter); Premier League 1998; FA Cup 1998. PFA Player of the Year 1998; Football Writers' Player of the Year 1998 (first man to win both awards in a season since John Barnes in 1988); BBC Goal of the Tournament Winner, 1998 World Cup.

Memorable Gunners' Match

The club's record signing didn't find the net in his first seven games, leading to criticism in the press. After all, 'The Iceman' had failed in Italy. But a double against Southampton in a 4-2 win (23.9.95) heralded his march towards becoming an all-time Arsenal great.

DID YOU KNOW

Bergkamp was named after Manchester United and Scotland legend Denis Law – but it is illegal in Holland to christen children using anything but standard spelling, so he had to be given the extra 'n'.

IT WAS ALWAYS going to be difficult for Bergkamp to follow his many triumphs of a memorable World Cup year. His goal in the quarter-final of France 98 against Argentina was three steps and just a couple of sublime touches to heaven. But the effort, coming hard on the heels of a punishing run-in to a Double-winning season with Arsenal, clearly took a great deal out of him, for it was a case of Dennis with little Menace for much of last term. Indeed it took him 10 Premiership games to get off the mark.

His morbid fear of flying yet again cost Arsenal his services in Europe. In previous years his absence cost them first-round UEFA Cup defeats against Borussia Monchengladbach and PAOK Salonika. Last term he ducked out of trips to Kiev and Panathinaikos in the Gunners' first Champions' League campaign.

'We are not the same team without Dennis,' admits Arsene Wenger, the Gunners boss. The truth is that they are not such a potent force without the Dutchman at his mercurial best.

His ball skills were honed during his time at the famed Ajax youth academy and it shows. He can take the ball with either foot, posesses instant control, wonderful awareness of his colleagues, a great eye for goal – and the ability to finish coolly under pressure.

The Dutchman had an unhappy time at Inter Milan, where he was expected to be the blue and black side of the football-mad city's version of Marco van Basten, sadly long since retired early through injury. But Bergkamp never settled, even though he won a UEFA Cup there, and was happy to make the £7m switch to London, signed by the short-lived Gunners boss Bruce Rioch.

Bergkamp brings the best out of his less high-profile team-mates with his unselfish running off the ball and passing ability. Ray Parlour says: 'I owe so much to Dennis. He can pick you out in a crowd and the ball is always right there in your stride. He's a fantastic player.'

Bergkamp has pledged to finish his career at Highbury and is always worth the ticket price. And the Highbury faithful will forgive him his penalty miss in the last minute of the Gunners' FA Cup semi-final replay with Manchester United.

The 1998 Footballer of the Year will surely win more trophies and accolades with the club.

Bergkamp added a Charity Shield win to his glittering career last season

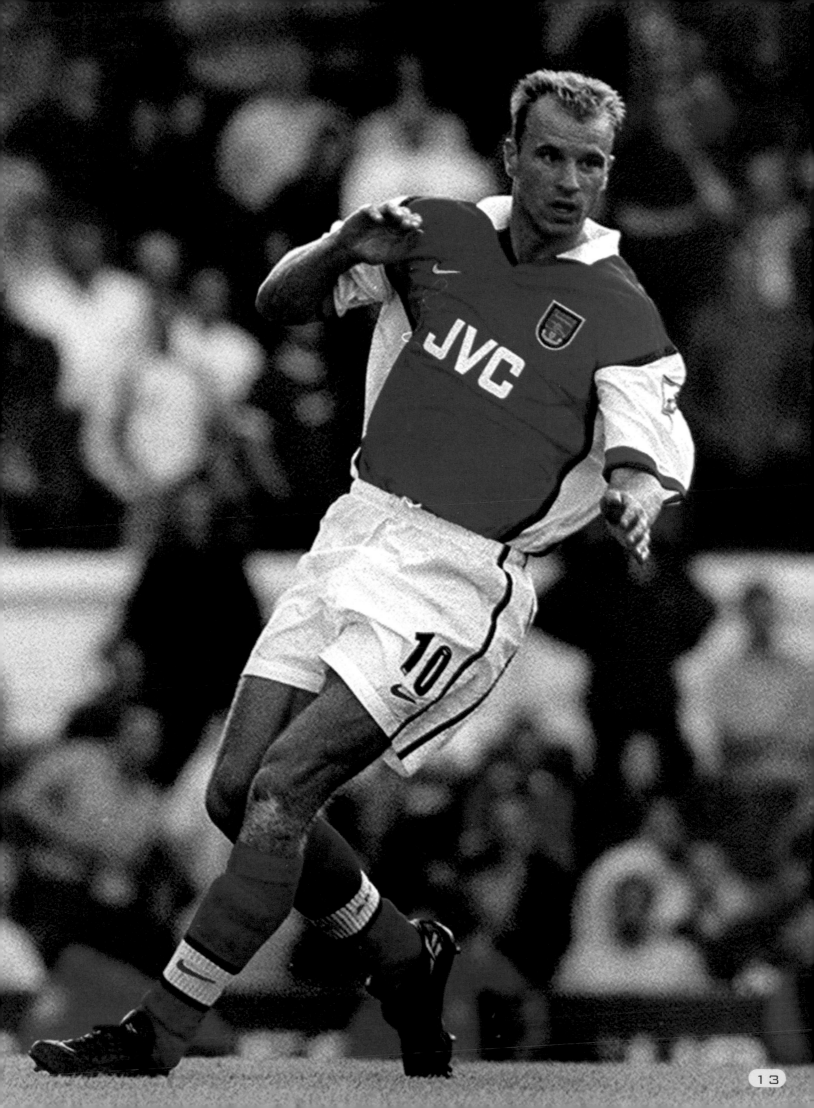

SOL CAMPBELL
TOTTENHAM HOTSPUR

STATS

Age	24	
Born	18 September 1974, Newham, London	
Size	6'2", 14st 4lbs	
Position	Central Defender	

Club	League Apps	League Goals
Tottenham	205	8

England International

25 appearances, 0 goals

Transfers

None – signed for Tottenham as trainee

Honours

Worthington Cup winner, 1999

Memorable Spurs' Match

1999 Worthington Cup Final v Leicester. Long-linked with a move away from White Hart Lane before George Graham arrived to build a proper defence around him, Campbell led by example as Tottenham won their first trophy since 1991.

SUCCESS doesn't faze Sol Campbell – but it is a happy new experience for the Spurs and England defensive giant coveted by some of Europe's biggest clubs.

It has been a long time coming for Sulzeer Jeremiah Campbell, to give him his full name. Sol was a pupil at the former FA School of Excellence at Lilleshall when Tottenham last reached a Wembley final – the 1991 FA Cup victory over Nottingham Forest. Since then, apart from the Jurgen Klinsmann-led season under Gerry Francis when Spurs reached the FA Cup semis, Campbell has been in the soup, as it were, with mid-table mediocrity or relegation dogfights.

England recognition brought him rare moments of escapism and of course for a split second in the World Cup he thought he had put England into the quarter-finals with an headed winner against Argentina, only for the goal to be ruled out for a foul by Alan Shearer.

'It was a big disappointment, of course, but it has made me more hungry to be successful with England,' he says. Campbell was an undoubted success in France, with some towering defensive work and eye-catching breaks upfield.

The likes of Lazio and Real Madrid have been following his career with interest. And, had Spurs' fortunes not picked up with the arrival of George Graham and his traditional assaults on Wembley, who knows?... Campbell might have de-camped in the summer. But all that has changed. 'We are doing well now,' he says. 'That is why I came to Tottenham.

'I have the same hunger for success as the fans. Now we are getting the right formula and a few things have been sorted out. But I don't have a crystal ball. I cannot say what will happen in years to come. All I can say is that I would never break a contract and I am a Tottenham man through and through.'

That will be music to the ears of all Spurs fans, who at last have a defender of the stature of some of the great White Hart Lane names of the past. Not since the 1970s, and the days of Welsh legend Mike England, have Spurs had a truly dominant player at the back. And what a difference it makes.

Graham's success at Arsenal was pinned on the foundation of his back four. Campbell is the cornerstone in Graham's new would-be dynasty.

DID YOU KNOW

Sol played in the same England Under-18 team as Robbie Fowler in 1993, helping them win the European Championships.

Campbell doing what he does best: clearing his lines against a West Ham attack

BENITO CARBONE

SHEFFIELD WEDNESDAY

STATS

Age	28
Born	14 August 1971, Bagnara Calabra, Italy
Size	5'6", 10st 8lbs
Position	Striker

Club	League Apps	League Goals
Torino	8	0
Reggina	31	5
Ascoli	28	6
Torino	28	3
Napoli	29	5
Inter Milan	32	2
Sheffield Wednesday	89	23

Transfers

Torino to Reggina, 1990
Inter Milan to Sheff Wed, October 1996, £3m

Honours

None

Memorable Owls' Match

Wednesday's 2-1 win at Everton in April 1999 effectively sealed their Premiership survival for another season – and it came about through Benito's opportunism. Twice opponents made mistakes, and twice the little Italian reacted like lightning to bring his team from 1-0 down to victory.

DID YOU KNOW

When Benito arrived at Hillsborough and was introduced to the crowd before a game, the club laid on a penalty shoot-out featuring a goalkeeper dressed up as Italian opera singer Luciano Pavarotti!

THE ONLY major bright spot in a hugely disappointing season for Sheffield Wednesday boss Danny Wilson last term was that brilliant Beni Carbone pledged his future to the club by signing a new deal.

Hillsborough's loyal following, starved of success, breathed a collective sigh, too, at the prospect of seeing more of the pocket-sized Italian's silky skills.

Wilson wants to build his Owls side around Carbone and is full of praise for his talents. 'When he gets hold of the ball people are frightened of him and give him time and space,' says Wilson. 'He has tremendous ability and vision and is also a great distributor of the ball.

'People tend to notice him only on the ball but he works hard when he does not have possession and creates his own space.

'He would be a huge asset to any club and that is why we had to tie him to a contract which keeps him at Hillsborough for as long as possible.'

Many thought Carbone would walk out on Wednesday after fellow countryman Paolo di Canio's departure. And he didn't hit it off with Wilson at first, especially when the boss labelled him a 'fancy dan' after a cup defeat against Cambridge.

Carbone admitted suffering homesickness following his £3m move from Inter Milan three years ago and he had been constantly linked with a return to one of his former clubs, Torino.

But now, it seems, he is fired up, loves his manager and living in Sheffield, and has been convinced that Wilson can get Wednesday ready to compete for honours.

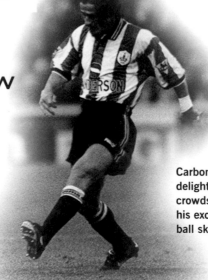

Carbone delights crowds with his exceptional ball skills

'It is a big club,' says Carbone. 'I came here to win things with them. I have a big respect for my manager and I believe we can go on to better things here now.'

Ron Atkinson, the Owls' former manager, was never won over by Carbone's ability, believing that the little maestro drifted out of too many games.

But predecessor David Pleat was a fan – he signed Carbone – and Wilson has placed his faith in the player, who has so often been the match-winner for Wednesday with his gift for going past players and finishing with deadly accuracy and poise.

Goal of the Month candidates are a speciality for this one...

ANDY COLE

MANCHESTER UNITED

DID YOU KNOW

Andy was sold to Bristol City by George Graham, who decided that Kevin Campbell (now of Everton) was the better striking prospect!

ANDY COLE hit the right note with his strike partner Dwight Yorke last season. Now the Manchester United man, blasted by former England boss Glenn Hoddle for his glaring misses in front of goal, aims to be a big hit in a different arena altogether.

Cole aims to complement life in the Theatre of Dreams with dreams of theatres – well, recording studios – having signed a music-making contract with Warner Brothers. His United team-mates thought David 'Mr Posh Spice' Beckham would be the first to move into the music world. One said: 'Andy's one of the quietest guys in the dressing room. We can't imagine him singing on Top Of The Pops!' Soul-fan Cole named his three-year-old son Devante after the lead singer of US band Jodeci and jumped at the chance of joining the same label as Shola Ama and Madonna.

On the pitch, Cole's goals were a prime ingredient in United's amazing season and his lethal partnership with Yorke frightened defences throughout Europe. Kenny Dalglish, whose pairing at Liverpool with Ian Rush was one of the deadliest seen in English football, says: 'Cole and Yorke would grace any team in the world. Their understanding seems to be almost telepathic.

'They are both very good players individually, but they have gone together to form a lethal partnership,' adds the new Celtic boss. 'They have a good relationship both on and off the pitch, and also enjoy seeing one another score goals. They are on the same wavelength.'

Cole capped a memorable year by resurrecting his England career against world champions France and scoring the goal that put United into the European Cup final. He had branded Glenn Hoddle 'a coward' in a remarkable outburst after the former England boss said Cole wasn't in his World Cup squad because he didn't put away enough chances. Cole said: 'I had kind of given up hope of playing for England again, but I don't regret what I said.'

Cole is one of the quietest in the dressing room but is lethal in front of goal

Remarkably, Hoddle's last act before he was axed was to forgive Cole and end his two-year international exile by naming him in his final squad.

'It was a surprise to be called up again after being out for so long,' said Cole, whose earlier caps – surprisingly only two – came as a substitute against Uruguay in 1995 and Italy in 1997.

Now if only we can cheat and get Yorke into the England team, too...

JOE COLE

WEST HAM UNITED

STATS

Age	17
Born	8 November 1981, London
Size	5'8", 10st 8lbs
Position	Midfielder

Club	League Apps	League Goals
West Ham	8	–

English

No International Appearance

Transfers

None, signed from trainee

Honours

FA Youth Cup 1999

Memorable Hammers' Match

It might have ended in a 4-1 defeat for his team, but Joe showed his potential when he made his league debut for West Ham against Manchester United in January, earning applause all round.

DID YOU KNOW

Joe Cole has until 5 January 2000 to break Michael Owen's record as the youngest England international this century

FEW CAREERS have been as widely heralded as that of Joe Cole. But West Ham legend Billy Bonds is able to put it into perspective.

'The way people have been carrying on, you'd think he'd run out there with a Superman cape on,' says Bonds. 'That is unfair on the lad.'

Cole bears a striking resemblance to another wonderkid we all know about – one with whom he starred for England's Under-16s –Michael Owen.

Cole's debut for the England Under-18's brought one goal and six assists, albeit against Andorra. And, while his arrival in the Hammers' first-team has not yet brought the same acclaim as Owen, few who have known him for years doubt that this boy will be in a class of his own.

Cole's former coach at Islington Boys, Terry Howard, recalls: 'When he had a trial with me I nearly had a heart-attack. He ran at an opponent in his own penalty box, back-flipped the ball over his head and kept on running. I tried to tell him there was a time and a place for that stuff. But when he did it again I said: "Do what you like, son".'

Rio Ferdinand likens Cole to Gazza. Alex Ferguson always mentions him when he talks to Hammers boss Harry Redknapp. Yet the fear, as ever with a major young talent, remains – will the breakneck pace of the ultra-competitive Premiership stifle the outrageous talent Cole possesses? It is a talent other sides, notably the Brazilians, are able to harness to rule the world.

'It's all very well doing his tricks in the playground, but I hope he doesn't try it on with Roy Keane,' says John Simon, a coach at Cole's old North London school.

What Cole does have on his side is that football is demanding more from its stars. They get big money – Cole isn't among the mega earners as yet, but he could well be a millionaire by the time he is 20 – and supporters who pay at the gate want their entertainers.

It's fashionable again to be a maverick like David Ginola or Gianfranco Zola.

Cole also has a shrewd manager in Redknapp, whose son Jamie was nursed along before breaking into the big-time.

Harry's game has been to keep Cole's feet on the ground. A gentle introduction, a high number on his shirt (26) and not too much cash in his pocket. He's very down to earth, friends say.

And this year, we should at last begin to discover what all the fuss has been about...

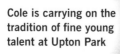

Cole is carrying on the tradition of fine young talent at Upton Park

MARCEL DESAILLY

CHELSEA

STATS

Age	30	
Born	7 September 1968, Accra, Ghana	
Size	6'2", 12st 7lbs	
Position	Midfielder/Defender	

Club	League Apps	League Goals
Nantes	162	5
Marseille	47	1
AC Milan	104	5
Chelsea	31	0

French International

Transfers Involving British Clubs

AC Milan to Chelsea, June 1998, £4.6m

Honours

World Cup 1998; European Cup 1993 (Marseille), 1994 (AC Milan), Runner-Up 1995; Italian Championship 1994, 1996; European Super Cup 1998 (Chelsea)

Memorable Blues' Match

Nine minutes from the end of the home Cup Winners' Cup game with FC Copenhagen, Marcel gave the ball away to gift the visitors a shock lead. But as time ran out, the Frenchman struck a 20-yard curling effort for his first goal for the club.

DID YOU KNOW

Marcel won the European Cup in 1993 with Marseille by beating AC Milan – the club he joined that summer and won the trophy with the next season.

MARCEL DESAILLY is Chelsea's Mr Versatile. He'll play anywhere for the Blues' cause. But few doubt the giant French World Cup winner's best position – in the centre of defence, alongside fellow countryman Frank Leboeuf.

'I am just as happy in either midfield or defence and it is up to the manager where I go,' says Desailly.

The man nicknamed The Rock, was a massive factor in Chelsea's improved defensive showing last season, when they conceded fewer goals in all competitions than any other Premiership side. Yet for much of the campaign, Desailly battled on despite Achilles tendon and knee problems.

Chelsea managed nine clean sheets in a club record unbeaten run, and of all Gianluca Vialli's signings, Desailly has looked the best value. Impressively, it was two-thirds of the way through the season before the Frenchman receive his first yellow card – a testament to his skill, pace and positional sense.

He is under no illusions about the challenge of Premiership football, despite his time in the hurly-burly of Italy. He says: 'In England the game is really hard and physical and it's not like that in Italy at all.

'I have been really surprised by that. While there is a lot of good quality in England, so much of the game is based on strength.

'People said it would be difficult for us to do well in the Premiership because we are all foreigners. They said we would never be able to play as a team, but I think we have shown everybody that we can.'

His game was honed in Serie A, where defences often dominate. 'When you play in defence, you have to be intelligent.

'I don't make many tackles and that helps me a lot. I use my pace to get possession rather than tackle. I don't get many yellow cards and it's a good statistic for me.'

Desailly has virtually won the lot, and is at the top of his profession. A World Cup winner's medal merely underlined his quality and standing on the global stage.

He says: 'I have won a lot in my career and I felt, that after winning medals in France and Italy, that it would be a positive experience to play in England.

'But I want to keep winning. That's why it is important for me to win the Premiership with Chelsea.'

Desailly gets one over Gazza

DION DUBLIN

ASTON VILLA

STATS

Age	30
Born	22 April 1969, Leicester
Size	6'2", 12st 4lbs
Position	Striker/Central defender

Club	League Apps	League Goals
Norwich City	–	–
Cambridge United	156	52
Manchester United	12	2
Coventry City	145	61
Aston Villa	24	11

England International

4 appearances, 0 goals

Transfers

Norwch to Cambridge Utd, August 1988, Free

Cambridge to Man Utd, August 1992, £1m

Man Utd to Coventry, September 1994, £2m

Coventry to Aston Villa, November 1998, £5.75m

Honours

Division Four Play-Offs 1990; Division Three Championship 1991

Memorable Villa Match

People questioned the wisdom of signing Dion, but he proved them wrong in his first match. He scored two contrasting goals. The first showed his poaching skills when a corner was gifted to him a few yards out, the second came at the end of a long run from his own half. 2-0, 35 minutes gone, and Villa beat Spurs 3-2.

DID YOU KNOW

Dion was at Manchester United when they won the 1993 and 1994 Premiership titles, but due to injury didn't play enough matches to qualify for a medal.

'MISS DWIGHT YORKE?' says Aston Villa boss John Gregory. 'Not at all. I'm more than happy with Dion Dublin.'

That might seem at odds with the evidence of last season, with Yorke's wonder goals show at home and in Europe for treble-winners Manchester United, and Dublin's loss of form after an explosive start for Villa.

But Gregory has no doubts that his £5.75m purchase of Dublin from Coventry more than offset the loss of Yorke to Old Trafford – with another £6m left over to throw into his team-building pot. And his view was backed up by Premiership bosses, who voted the move the best value transfer of the season.

Gregory says Yorke was going stale at Villa Park: 'As far as I'm concerned, all the jerseys hang together, but his wasn't on the same washing line. He no longer wanted to wear the jersey, and that tipped the balance. In three or four months, I doubt whether he would have been in the team.'

Dublin appeared to have been a fixture at Highfield Road, where his multi-talents were deployed at both ends of the field to great effect – often the thread on which City's Premiership survival clung. 'We were not prolific scorers until Dion arrived,' adds Gregory. 'I still can't believe Coventry let him go. I feel I have an absolute bargain – if you can call £5.75m a bargain.'

For Sky Blues, Dublin was used as a centre-back or an out-and-out striker. It was as the latter that the Leicester-born 30-year-old was capped three times for England under Glenn Hoddle and was unlucky to be left out of the 22 for the World Cup finals.

Whatever position he plays, Dublin is always a danger around the box, especially from set plays.

The irony of Yorke's departure to United is not lost on him – for Dublin had a spell at Old Trafford in 1992, moving for £1m from Cambridge United. But his time there was wrecked by a broken leg and he only made 12 appearances.

Intelligent and articulate, Dublin lives in Stratford, home of the Royal Shakespeare Company... apt really, because on the football field he is a class act.

Dublin made an explosive start to his Aston Villa career with a brace of goals

JASON EUELL

WIMBLEDON

DID YOU KNOW

As well as costing Liverpool the championship in 1997, in the very next match Jason scored the goal that relegated Sunderland!

Euell laps up some of that famous Wimbledon team spirit

JASON EUELL has saved Wimbledon a fortune in the transfer market – and football probably saved him from a life of petty crime, he says.

Euell believes he can become only the third Wimbledon star to play for England after Warren Barton and John Fashanu. But that is a far cry from school pitches around his native Brixton, where he might have been tempted to take an altogether different 'career' path.

'Thieving and drugs were quite a temptation,' says Euell. 'But I had set my mind on becoming a footballer. It was difficult to turn a blind eye to some of the things that went on. A lot of friends from school didn't and now they regret that.'

Euell and team-mate Carl Cort both came through the Dons' thriving youth ranks, though it was the former who got his big break first, scoring with an overhead kick on his debut against Southampton two years ago. 'That was probably the best feeling I've ever had. We were losing 1-0 and when it went in I was so excited.'

Since his early days as an out and out striker, he has been used in a more withdrawn role – but he hasn't lost his eye for goal. And, while fellow Dons, Robbie Earle and Marcus Gayle, switched their allegiance to Jamaica after being ignored by England, Under-21 striker Euell is convinced he can earn his first full cap without having to leave the club like Dennis Wise and Keith Curle.

'I don't know why Wimbledon players don't get selected for England. I don't think it matters which club you are at. If you're good enough then you'll get selected wherever you are,' says Euell, now 22.

Born in London's Elephant and Castle and pursued by numerous clubs as a teenager, he elected to join unfashionable Wimbledon 'because they give youth a chance. I don't base myself on anyone. It's important to be yourself but I did look up to players like Glenn Hoddle, John Barnes and Ian Wright because they were good ball players.'

Former manager Joe Kinnear described Euell as "the next Robbie Earle". He added: 'Jason got better and better as last season went on. 'Never mind the three R's. In football, it's the three A's. Attitude, ability and application.

'Wimbledon has them in abundance. Jason is a jewel – a star in the making.'

RIO FERDINAND
WEST HAM UNITED

DID YOU KNOW

Rio and England teammate Les Ferdinand didn't know they were cousins until a chance meeting between other relatives from the island of St Lucia revealed the connection.

Ferdinand doubles up with teammate Julian Dicks to snub out an opposition attack

LIFE IS never simple when your name is Rio. And you're from Peckham. Rio Ferdinand – it sounds like a wind-up by another of Peckham's finest – Del Boy.

Even the lad himself, one of England's outstanding young footballing talents, has found it a bit odd coming to terms with seeing his name in lights and hearing the fans chant his name.

'I used to watch *Match of the Day* every week to see if I was on it. When I was on for the first time it was brilliant. Now I only watch if I've scored,' he says. The warmth of the Wembley crowd that greeted his England debut as a substitute against Cameroon in 1998 clearly struck a chord. As Ferdy warmed up on the touchline, the chants for him to come on grew, sending shivers down his spine.

But he had better get used to it. The comparisons with West Ham icon Bobby Moore may be an unfair burden – but if the caps fit... 'Yeah, there is some similarity,' Rio says mischievously. 'The claret and blue...'

And those colours seem to run through young Rio's veins, despite frequent rumours of Harry Redknapp cashing in by selling his most prized asset (even allowing for Frank Lampard and Joe Cole).

Rio shows such a great maturity for his tender age – not yet 21 – and so far his greatest influence in what promises to be a wonderful career may be the games he didn't play.

He was there in France with England at the World Cup. And while he didn't kick a ball (or an Argentinian) in anger, the experience cemented his desire and focus, as well as showing him first hand the level of determination and concentration needed to fulfil his destiny.

He is blessed with wonderful athleticism (he could have been a gymnast), a wonderful positional sense and times his tackles to perfection. He operates as a centre-half for his club but he could become the pivotal part of England's future as a sweeper.

Rio – the name sounds Brazilian and there's a bit of the samba rhythm to the way he plays. With another ten like him, perhaps we could finally give Ronaldo and Co a lesson. And see the 'new Bobby Moore' get his hands on the biggest prize of all – the World Cup.

DUNCAN FERGUSON

NEWCASTLE UNITED

STATS

Age	27
Born	27 December 1971, Stirling
Size	6'3", 13st 5lbs
Position	Striker

Club	League Apps	League Goals
Dundee United	77	27
Glasgow Rangers	14	2
Everton	116	37
Newcastle United	7	2

Scottish International

7 appearances, 0 goals

Transfers

Dundee Utd to Rangers, July 1993, £4m

Rangers to Everton, October 1994, £4.4m

Everton to Newcastle, November 1998, £8m

Honours

Scottish League 1994; Scottish League Cup 1994; FA Cup 1995; FA Cup runner-up 1999

Memorable Toon Match

The 3-1 win over Wimbledon in November 1998 was Duncan's debut. Ruud Gullit's side were level at 1-1 with nearly an hour gone when he opened his account with a drive. Then to round the game off in the 90th minute he scored from a Keith Gillespie corner with one of his trademark headers.

DID YOU KNOW

As well as football, Duncan is very keen on another sport – though it couldn't be more different. He keeps racing pigeons!

WHEN THE Magpies slipped past Spurs to reach their second successive FA Cup Final, history repeated itself for Duncan Ferguson.

The giant Scot's sense of *deja vu* was uncanny. Four years earlier, within months of joining Everton, Ferguson had a long-term injury. 'I had a groin operation and came back in time to play in the FA Cup final,' he recalls.

Last season he had ten weeks on the sidelines with a similar injury and operation – and returned in time for the Wembley showdown with Manchester United. Ferguson should be used to spells out of the game. His colourful past has seen him suspended, injured – even jailed. But he says it doesn't get any easier.

'I was brought in to do a job alongside Alan Shearer. But the pair of us had our injuries and the frustration was unbelievable.'

The 27-year-old picked up his injury at Liverpool on Boxing Day, not long after the transfer he never wanted. 'I felt sick when Everton told me I was being sold for financial reasons,' he said. 'I was happy and settled on Merseyside.'

Before Ferguson's injury, he and Shearer, the £23m pairing that manager Ruud Gullit staked his future on, had teamed up only twice.

Gullit believes they are a duo to die for, complementing each other's strengths. Ferguson, at six feet four, is of course, awesome in the air (Shearer is pretty handy in that department, too!), but he is also very mobile for a big man, with good pace and close control.

He was idolised at Everton, where manager Howard Kendall made him captain. Big Dunc responded typically with a hat-trick of headed goals against Bolton. In a career that began at Dundee United and continued more controversially at Glasgow Rangers, Ferguson has often been the centre of attention because of his combative nature.

But away from the game he is a private person, who seldom gives interviews.

Scots fans wish he would end his long-standing feud with his FA – he hasn't played since a World Cup qualifier against Estonia – and make himself available for Craig Brown's side. He sat out the World Cup and got married instead.

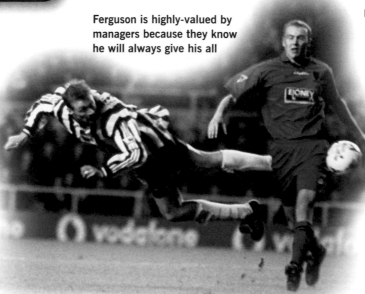

Ferguson is highly-valued by managers because they know he will always give his all

TORE ANDRE FLO

CHELSEA

STATS

Age	26
Born	15 June 1973, Strin, Norway
Size	6'4", 13st 8lbs
Position	Striker

Club	League Apps	League Goals
Sogndal	22	5
Tromso	25	18
Brann	40	28
Chelsea	64	21

Norwegian International

Transfers Involving British Clubs

Brann Bergen to Chelsea, August 1997, £300,000

Honours

European Cup Winners' Cup 1998; League Cup 1998; European Super Cup 1998

Memorable Blues' Match

Chelsea faced a tough away game in the quarter-final of the 1998 Cup Winners' Cup, against Real Betis of Spain. But Tore Andre scored twice in the first 12 minutes to as good as win the tie.

DID YOU KNOW

Tore Andre's elder brother, Jostein, also played in England. He was at Sheffield United in the early 1990s, and played for the Norwegian national team, helping them beat England and reach the 1994 World Cup.

HE FLEW IN and, for a time, Flo seemed sure to fly off. But the giant Norwegian international has finally settled at Stamford Bridge, signing a five-year deal securing the £10m-rated striker's future in west London.

Flo's future had been uncertain because he was unhappy with Gianluca Vialli's policy of rotating his squad. He wanted a regular starting slot and found himself behind Brian Laudrup, Pierluigi Casiraghi and even the manager himself.

Flo had been set to join Everton when former Toffees boss Joe Royle found himself strapped for cash, unable to find the £2.6m to prise him from Brann Bergen.

It was his performances for Brann against Liverpool in the UEFA Cup that first brought him to the attention of Premiership clubs.

Chelsea stepped in and paid a bargain £300,000 for the last three months of his contract and Flo looked a great investment when he scored twice as Norway shocked world champions Brazil with a 4-2 win prior to last year's World Cup. Just for good measure, he scored against the samba boys again in France before Norway crashed out to Italy.

And he wasn't slow to make his mark in the Premiership, scoring successive hat-tricks, including one against Spurs in a record 6-1 win at White Hart Lane.

His outings have since been staggered, and he has probably suffered more than his rivals for a starting place through not playing a consistent long run of matches.

But he is confident enough of Chelsea's potential to be a European power to want to pledge his future to the club. And, after the Blues' recent successful runs in the Cup-winners' Cup, they could yet prove a handful in the enlarged Champions' League. With Flo to the fore.

His first medal came as a substitute against Middlesbrough in the Coca-Cola Cup final and he became a big favourite with Chelsea fans as he shared in the 1998 Cup-Winners' Cup success.

'That's why I came here – to win things. I was never in any doubt that I would do well here. And I think it will continue to get better,' Flo predicts.

Flo is aiming to make his mark in the Champions' League

ROBBIE FOWLER

LIVERPOOL

STATS

Age	24	
Born	9 April 1975	
	Liverpool	
Size	5'11", 11st 10lbs	
Position	Striker	

Club	League Apps	League Goals
Liverpool	184	106

England International

8 appearances, 2 goals

Transfers

None – signed as trainee.

Honours

Coca Cola Cup winner 1995; FA Cup Runner-Up 1996; PFA Young Player Of The Year 1995 and 1996.

Memorable Reds' Match

Liverpool 5 Fulham 0, September 1993. Scored on his debut against the same opponents in a 3-1 away win in the Coca Cola Cup, but really announced his talent by scoring all five in the second leg.

ALL-ACTION HERO Robbie Fowler is a man of contradictions. He is Liverpool's natural successor to Ian Rush and is described by Michael Owen as his dream playing partner. Yet Fowler never seems to lose his capacity for attracting the wrong kind of headlines. He has probably suffered most from the Anfield 'Spice Boys' reputation, and had more than his fair share of scrapes.

But he also has a caring side. He was accused of being greedy in asking Liverpool to stump up an enormous new salary or he'd leave Anfield. Some said he had forgotten his roots in hard-nosed Toxteth. Yet he'd also come out publicly with a T-shirt slogan in favour of striking Liverpool dockers in their pay dispute – and got fined for his troubles.

Talks of a big-money move to Arsenal persisted until he signed a new deal that will keep him at the club he loves. Liverpool Football Club is in his blood.

Last season did not start well for Fowler, who has seen his place as Kop icon overshadowed by the brilliance of Michael Owen. He returned to action in the autumn, ahead of schedule after seven months on the sidelines with injury. But soon picked up where he left off – scoring goals and making headlines.

His first meaningful contribution was to provide the inch-perfect pass for Owen to score against the Slovaks, Kosice, in the UEFA Cup.

It was an aerial collision with Everton goalkeeper Thomas Myhre near the end of the February 1998 derby meeting at Anfield which left him nursing badly damaged knee ligaments and facing a long haul back to fitness which was initially expected to drag on until Christmas.

But Fowler showed his professionalism and dedication in the gym, to come back almost five weeks early. The injury possibly cost him a place in England's World Cup squad, yet he was philosophical about it: 'It could have been worse. At least much of the time out was during the summer when most of the lads were around and were able to help keep my spirits up,' he said.

Not that 24-year-old Fowler ever seems short on spirit – or goals. His craft in front of the net brought the curtain down on Liverpool legend Rush's Anfield reign, and he could now go on to rewrite the Kop record books.

DID YOU KNOW

Robbie Fowler, like his fellow Liverpool stars Ian Rush, Steve McManaman and Michael Owen, was an Everton fan when he was growing up!

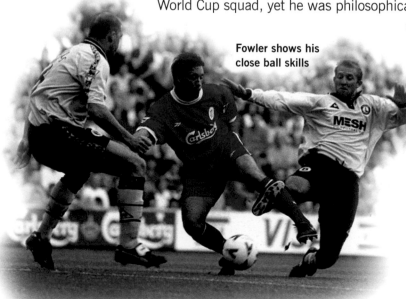

Fowler shows his close ball skills

RYAN GIGGS
MANCHESTER UNITED

STATS

Age	25	
Born	29 November 1973, Cardiff	
Size	5'11", 10st 10lbs	
Position	Midfielder	

Club	League Apps	League Goals
Manchester United	260	53

Welsh International

22 appearances, 5 goals

Transfers

None, signed as schoolboy

Honours

European Cup 1999; Premiership 1993, 1994, 1996, 1997, 1999; FA Cup 1994, 1996, 1999, Runner-Up 1995; League Cup 1992, Runner-Up 1994; PFA Young Player Of The Year 1992, 1993

Memorable United Match

The first leg of Manchester United's Champions League Semi-Final with Juventus seemed to be lost, with United a goal down in stoppage time, as they had been for much of the match. But Ryan scored a late equaliser to keep the dream alive. It may not have been as spectacular as his goal in the FA Cup semi against Arsenal, but it was every bit as important.

DID YOU KNOW

Ryan Giggs may be a Welsh international, but he used to captain England schoolboys! His father, Danny Wilson, also represented England – but at rugby league.

WITH ONE MOMENT of sublime skill, Ryan Giggs finally became the player he has threatened to become for a long time – and cemented his place in the annals of the game for all time.

You can never get tired of watching it. He picked the ball up just inside the Arsenal half, with seconds left in a tense, enthralling FA Cup semi-final replay, and arrowed towards goal. He left a trail of defenders in his wake and tricked two more with a remarkable double shuffle of his feet and sway of the hips. He fended off a desperate lunge from Tony Adams and then beat the imposing figure of David Seaman. As the ball thumped the back of the net, Giggs wheeled away waving his shirt above his head. It was the moment that Alex Ferguson, the Manchester United manager, believed Giggs and his team-mates became 'gods'.

Giggs was the first of Fergie's home-grown crop to become an Old Trafford legend, alongside the likes of Eric Cantona as United laid a 26-year hoodoo by winning the Premiership title in 1993. Since then, it has been glory, glory all the way, though Giggs has often been criticised for not producing goods from the top drawer over a sustained period.

Injuries kept him out of two title run-ins and undermined their hopes of European success. He's missed more games for Wales than he has appeared in for his adopted country.

Giggs' value to the United side cannot be understated. Diego Simeone, the Argentina international who famously clashed with David Beckham in the last World Cup, says: 'United are not quite the same threat without Giggs. He can make things happen out of nothing.' Giggs was burdened in his earliest days at Old Trafford by constant comparison with George Best. Ferguson says: 'He will never be a Best. George was unique. But so is Ryan.'

When it comes to the footballer's traditional hallmark of ability – medals on the table – Giggs outscores Best by a mile. Five Premiership titles, three FA Cups and now, they each have a European Cup.

Giggs is now his own man, a very wealthy one, too. He has a car collection to die for, including a custom-made Jeep, a limited-edition Ferrari Maranello 550 – as well as a Colin McRae-style Subaru rally monster. Kind of apt, really, given that rally-like route to glory against the Gunners...

Giggs' blistering pace has been crucial in Man United's success

DAVID GINOLA
TOTTENHAM HOTSPUR

STATS

Age	32
Born	25 January 1967, Gossin, France
Size	5'11", 11st 10lbs
Position	Midfielder

Club	League Apps	League Goals
Toulon	81	4
Matra Racing	29	7
Racing Paris 1	32	1
Brest	50	10
Paris St Germain	115	32
Newcastle	58	6
Tottenham	64	9

French International

17 appearances, 3 goals

Transfers

PSG to Newcastle, July 1995, £2.5m

Newcastle to Spurs, July 1997, £2m

Honours

French championship 1994, French Cup 1993, 1995, French League Cup 1995 (all PSG), finalist 1990 (Racing Paris 1), Coca-Cola Cup 1999

Memorable Spurs Match

Tottenham's FA Cup victory over Barnsley this season saw David score one of the great individual goals, running through the defence from 40 yards out by the touchline before stroking the ball home. Magnificent!

DID YOU KNOW

In October 1997, David came first and third in Match Of The Day's Goal Of The Month competition the first time anyone had filled two of the top three slots.

FORGET RONALDO and even World Player of the Year Zinedine Zidane – David Ginola is the best of the lot! That was the view of Dutch legend Johann Cruyff last season. 'He's got to be the most exciting player to watch at the moment.

'On his day he is as good as anybody and he is having a lot of those sort of days right now,' said Cruyff. 'He is a tremendous talent and it is easy to see why people in England have taken him to their hearts.'

Tottenham's French wizard had a wonderful season winning dual Player of the Year awards – putting paid to speculation that he would be the first high-profile casualty of George Graham's reign at White Hart Lane.

Under Christian Gross, Ginola was the only player worth the entrance money. Now, with Spurs on song, Ginola is merely the orchestra leader – and a present day Tottenham legend to set alongside Greaves, Hoddle, Gascoigne and Lineker.

Ginola's move to Spurs surprised many. He was easily dismissed as a luxury suitable only for the sort of suicide soccer practiced by Kevin Keegan's Newcastle. But oh how Keegan and England could have done with Ginola's talents – especially as France are so richly endowed – or foolish enough – to ignore the man with the flowing locks and model looks.

Liverpool's Gerard Houllier was in charge of France when Ginola last played for his country, a World Cup qualifier against Bulgaria in 1993. Houllier blamed Ginola for giving away the goal that cost France a place in the USA finals and he has been a national outcast since.

Many, though, among them Ruud Gullit, Keegan's successor at Newcastle, believed Ginola should have been in the World champions' squad in 1998.

It is difficult to pick out any single moments of Ginola magic for special mention – you could compile a whole Goal of the Month competition from his Tottenham scrapbook. But he single-handedly destroyed Leeds in a memorable FA Cup replay, topping it off with a wonderful volley from outside the box to seal the win.

Dangerously effective when he is show the line by his full-back, Ginola is deadly when allowed to cut in side and unload his wicked, curling shot across the keeper.

He was less effective as Spurs beat Leicester to lift the Coca-Cola Cup. But he's been a huge tonic for the long-suffering Spurs supporters.

Ginola is expert at weaving his way through defences

SHAY GIVEN
NEWCASTLE UNITED

STATS

Age	23	
Born	24 April 1976, Lifford, Republic of Ireland	
Size	6'0", 11st 8lbs	
Position	Goalkeeper	

Club	League Apps	League Goals
Blackburn	2	–
Swindon (loan)	5	–
Sunderland (loan)	17	–
Newcastle	55	–

Irish International

23 appearances

Transfers

Blackburn to Newcasrle, July 1997, £1.5m

Honours

FA Cup Runner-Up, 1998 and 1999

Memorable Magpies' Match

Newcastle's 1999 FA Cup Semi-Final win over Tottenham saw Shay in magnificent form, keeping a clean sheet to help his side reach Wembley for the second year in a row.

DID YOU KNOW

Shay always takes care to look all around himself now. Playing against Coventry once, he put the ball on the ground to take a run-up, not noticing that Dion Dublin was standing behind him and stole the ball and put it in the empty net!

Given has given Newcastle much-needed steel at the back

SHAY GIVEN was brought in by Kenny Dalglish to be the Newcastle No.1. But the young Irishman knows that under Ruud Gullit he faces a big fight for his place. The talented goalkeeper, who has been inspirational in the Magpies' successive FA Cup Finals knows that understudy Steve Harper is capable of keeping him on the sidelines for even longer.

'I watch Steve on the training ground every day and I know exactly what he can do,' says the Republic of Ireland international. 'I can't take my place for granted and that helps me stay on my toes.'

Given's £1.5m move from Blackburn was one of Dalglish's first deals and he has learned much from the man he idolised.

'One of the most important things Kenny told me was not to get too down about defeat or to get too high in victory.'

Keeping his emotions in check does not come easily, though. Given famously burst into tears when the Republic of Ireland failed in their World Cup qualifying play-off in Belgium.

'We just didn't perform on the day,' he recalls.

He had been a frustrated understudy to Tim Flowers at Blackburn when he joined Newcastle after a loan spell at Sunderland. But he spent three months on the bench as Shaka Hislop's understudy. And he was only recalled to the Newcastle team when Hislop became involved in a contractual row with Dalglish.

Even though he is six feet tall, Given struggles occasionally in the air. But he is a brilliant, athletic shot-stopper and Ireland boss Mick McCarthy has been quick to support his international claims, giving him most of his 23 senior caps, even when Given was not first choice with his club.

Given earned his spurs in the Cup semi-final with Tottenham, with a display that suggested it would take something special to beat him. And, at just 23, he is sure to be in a position to win many major honours.

JOHN HARTSON

WIMBLEDON

STATS

Age	24	
Born	5 April 1975, Swansea	
Size	6'1", 14st 6lbs	
Position	Striker	

Club	League Apps	League Goals
Luton	54	11
Arsenal	53	14
West Ham	60	24
Wimbledon	14	2

Welsh International

15 appearances, 2 goals

Transfers

Luton to Arsenal, January 1995, £2.5m
Arsenal to West Ham, February 1997, £3.2m
West Ham to Wimbledon, January 1999, £7.5m
.

Honours

None

Memorable Dons' Match

John scored his first goal for Wimbledon against Newcastle in April 1999, to earn his new team a valuable point with a typical poachers' goal.

DID YOU KNOW

John's transfer to Arsenal was a record fee received for Luton; his move to West Ham was a record fee paid by them; then West Ham received a record fee and Wimbledon paid one when he made that move.

CONTROVERSY seems attached to John Hartson. Often in the headlines for his fiery moments on the field, the red-headed Welshman stunned football when he made a massive £7m move to supposed Premiership paupers Wimbledon last year.

Hot-headed and temperamental are just two words frequently used to describe Hartson. His famous training-ground brawl with team-mate Eyal Berkovic signalled the end of his brief spell at West Ham, who were happy to cash in when Joe Kinnear, the Dons' former boss, came calling.

West Ham saw themselves as the winners in the deal, almost doubling their money on the striker they signed from Arsenal in February 1997 for £3.2m.

Hartson's physical presence is his best weapon, though there were signs last season that in trying to curb his on-the-field excesses, he has lost some of his potency in front of goal.

The 24-year-old Welsh international says he is a much calmer figure since the birth last spring on his daughter, Rebecca. 'I'm absolutely thrilled to be a dad and I'm so proud. It's the best feeling in the world. It put everything into perspective for me.'

Following his move to Selhurst Park he lost almost a stone in intensive workouts, clearly determined to justify the massive fee the Dons paid for him.

Kinnear, whose season was curtailed with heart problems, never had any doubts about Hartson's ability to keep Wimbledon in the Premiership top ten and prove a perennial pain to their rivals.

'I always wanted to sign him, right from when he started out at Luton. Vinnie Jones kept on at me about him.

Hartson has a poor reputation with refs

'John is a top-quality striker who has proven himself at the highest level. He's still young but he is experienced and skillful and will be a great asset for a long time, Kinnear said.

'People might wonder at the size of the fee but the club has half-a-dozen players worth that much and more in my squad. The only difference is that I have not sold them and will not be doing so.

'We have been building a good young squad that can take Wimbledon into the new millennium challenging for honours and going for Europe. John will be a big part of that.'

JIMMY FLOYD HASSELBAINK
LEEDS UNITED

HE HAS yet to visit the street that bears his name back in Surinam. The Dutch colony has named many streets after its famous sons – Rijkaard, Gullit, Seedorf, Davids. Hasselbaink Street – it has a certain ring to it. And if the man known simply as Jimmy continues to make headlines at the same rate, they'll soon be naming something more substantial after him.

Jimmy's real name is Jerrel Floyd Hasselbaink. He got his more familiar moniker when he was playing in Portugal for Campomaiorense. The club president re-named the athletic Dutch international striker in order to hush up his move to the club following a troubled spell with AZ Alkmaar, in Holland.

The move to Leeds surprised many Premiership fans, though scouts at Werder Bremen and Napoli had seen enough to share the interest shown in him by George Graham. Hasselbaink had a reputation for scoring goals but was also known for not being the most mild mannered of players.

'I've had my fair share of scrapes,' admits Hasselbaink. 'I've done some stupid things, like going in for crazy tackles and getting into silly situations with other players. But I'm more together now, much more patient.'

The changes began under Graham, whom he says was 'the hardest man I've played for'. He marked his first English season with 22 goals, to earn a call-up for the Dutch squad for the World Cup in France, the highlight of his career so far, especially when he was in the side that opened up against Belgium.

But he warns that David O'Leary is no soft option. 'We've clashed once or twice, but he's made it clear he's the boss and we don't have any problems.' O'Leary has been happy to lean on Hasselbaink's new maturity as he leads a young front line with the potential to be the best. 'Alan Smith and Harry Kewell have been getting the headlines, but we have a number of other excellent young players coming through at Elland Road,' says Hasselbaink.

Hasselbaink is one of a number of players that promise great things for Leeds

DID YOU KNOW

Jimmy Floyd Hasselbaink has the longest name in the Premiership!

DARREN HUCKERBY

COVENTRY CITY

DID YOU KNOW

Darren shares his birthday with William Shakespeare – and the England hopeful and the country's most famous playwright were both born on St George's Day.

THE COVENTRY CITY FLIER – that's Darren Huckerby, one of the quickest, trickiest strikers in the Premiership. And, according to World Cup winner Frank Leboeuf, of Chelsea, it is staggering that he isn't already a fixture in the England squad.

The Sky Blues, who have had to sell their best stars in order to survive in the Premiership, value Huck enormously and say he is not leaving Highfield Road. Not even for £10m.

But the Nottingham-born youngster has become used to rejection. Capped four times at Under-21 level and once for the B side, he has yet to figure for the full side – and it was England coach Kevin Keegan who sold him to Coventry in 1996 for a bargain £1m. Newcastle did at least more than double their money on the deal, having paid Lincoln £400,000 for him 18 months earlier. The Magpies didn't have a reserve side at the time and impatient Huckerby was not content to wait for his chance at St James'.

At 23, Huckerby still has time to make his mark for his country. He has frequently given quality defenders like Leboeuf, Sol Campbell and Tony Adams major headaches with his raw pace and close control. He has learnt to time his runs better and no longer gets caught offside as frequently as during his early matches in the Premiership. Coventry chairman Bryan Richardson says: 'We got him for £800,000 but he has got to be worth £10m now.

'His speed, control and strength make him one of the most feared strikers in the country right now,' he adds.

It was Dion Dublin's £5.75m move to Aston Villa last season that breathed new life into Huckerby and strike partner Noel Whelan. Huckerby was soon into double figures with his goals return.

Richardson says: 'Darren is a more exciting player than Dion.'

Yet manager Gordon Strachan says Huckerby is still far from the finished article, saying he needs to be more consistent.

'He goes from being a world beater to a carpet beater,' says Strachan.

'Darren can do things on his day that nobody else in football can do. But he needs to find a more consistent level of performance.'

If given space to move, Huckerby can be a devastating striker

STEFFAN IVERSEN
TOTTENHAM HOTSPUR

STATS

Age	22	
Born	10 November 1976, Oslo, Norway	
Size	6'1", 11st 8lbs	
Position	Striker	

Club	League Apps	League Goals
Rosenborg	25	10
Tottenham	56	15

Norwegian International

Transfers
Rosenborg to Spurs, December 1996, £2.7m

Honours
Norwegian Championship 1996; League Cup 1999

Memorable Spurs' Match
Steffen settled Tottenham's Worthington Cup Semi-Final with Wimbledon. His second leg winner at Selhurst Park was an excellent lob over keeper Neil Sullivan, seeing his team through to Wembley.

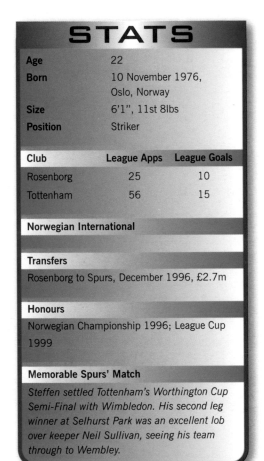

DID YOU KNOW

Steffen played in the Champions League when he was at Rosenborg, and scored for them against 1995 English champions Blackburn.

HE'S ONE of Norway's golden strike trio. Along with Ole Gunnar Solskjaer and Tore Andre Flo, Steffen Iversen has helped to shoot his country into prime position for a major Euro2000 challenge.

At Spurs, injuries have all too often reduced his potential to fully outgun the man he was bought to replace – Teddy Sheringham. Spurs Director of Football David Pleat believes Iversen has what it takes to win a place in the hearts of Spurs fans and threaten Teddy's amazing run of 99 goals in five years at White Hart Lane.

'Steffen is determined to make a go of his career in England and I believe he is set for a golden future,' says Pleat.

Quick and mobile, the athletically-built blond Viking striker was signed from Rosenborg, then the Norwegian champions, for £2.7m by Gerry Francis. It was said around a dozen top clubs had been trailing him. But Spurs were the only club to table a decent offer and Iversen and his family were sold on the club instantly. The irony is that Francis bought Iversen to help at a time of injury crisis – and yet the 22-year-old Oslo-born forward has been beset by a string of unfortunate knocks and bumps since his debut against Coventry.

He missed a spell last season when he broke his jaw following a collision with Liverpool goalkeeper David James.

And returning from international duties in the past with further injuries has not helped him win favour or a regular place alongside Chris Armstrong or Les Ferdinand. There are similarities to Sheringham in Iversen's game, not least his ability to pick a pass and to use space intelligently. He is now playing under his third manager at Spurs following the departure of Francis and the short-lived reign of Christian Gross.

But there are signs that George Graham, the new man in charge, likes Iversen's raw talent and believes he can make the player a polished product by applying some of the formulas he employed with Arsenal.

Iversen is sure to grow in confidence after Spurs' return to trophy glory, winning the Coca-Cola Cup last term. And his experience in Europe with Rosenborg and now his country will aid Spurs in their UEFA Cup campaign.

Iverson has experienced glory with Spurs in the Coca-Cola Cup

JULIAN JOACHIM

ASTON VILLA

STATS

Age	24
Born	20 September 1974, Peterborough
Size	5'6", 12st 0lbs
Position	Striker

Club	League Apps	League Goals
Leicester City	99	25
Aston Villa	88	26

England

No international appearances

Transfers

Leicester to Aston Villa, February 1996, £1.5m

Honours

None

Memorable Villa Match

In John Gregory's third match in charge, Julian sealed all three points with the only goal of the game at Stamford Bridge against Chelsea. His second half strike not only lifted the team closer to safety, but gave Julian the best possible lift in the eyes of the new manager.

OF ALL the strikers in John Gregory's Villa arsenal, Julian Joachim benefited most from the £12m sale of Dwight Yorke to Manchester United.

Yorke's move to Old Trafford enabled Gregory to strengthen his squad with the signings of Paul Merson and Dion Dublin.

And, while that was a major threat to Joachim's tenure at Villa Park, the former Leicester and Young England star responded magnificently as Gregory's boys set the early Premiership pace last term.

For a time, Joachim was fourth-choice striker behind Yorke, Stan Collymore and Savo Milosevic but he emerged from the supporting cast to strike up a handy partnership with Dublin.

Joachim, now 24, and so far yet to fully live up to the promise he showed as a teenager, said: 'Dwight is an excellent player but we proved we could cope without him and that we were not just a one-man show.

'People thought we would struggle to score without him but we proved them all wrong. 'In many ways, Dwight going was a good move for the club.'

Joachim missed few games – a rare experience for the Peterborough-born striker in recent seasons both at Villa Park and Leicester, whom he joined in 1992 as a trainee. He had expected much from the switch to Villa, but Ian Taylor's form kept him restricted to the bench for long spells. He still managed to equal Collymore's eight-goal return in Stan The Man's first season with his 'dream club'.

Joachim has been nicknamed 'the little Brazilian' because of his pace and trickery on the ball. And, after his best season at Villa Park, Gregory put a £6m price-tag on him to keep other clubs at bay.

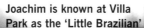

Joachim is known at Villa Park as the 'Little Brazilian'

His pace and durability offers his manager various options – he has been used out wide and in midfield as well as in a central striking role.

'I'm really enjoying my football again and it's great to have earned a regular place in the side,' he says. 'Dion is great to play with and he's been a revelation since he came to the club.'

Joachim made the move across the Midlands because he wants to win things and make the step up to the senior England side after nine outings for the Under-21s.

A Premiership crown would do very nicely now, says Joachim. 'People have not been taking us seriously at all at Villa but I think we proved last season that we can compete with the best teams in the League.

'Hopefully now we can go on from that and we can win the title.'

DID YOU KNOW

Julian showed just how important he is to Villa by being their top scorer for the 1998-99 campaign.

ROY KEANE
MANCHESTER UNITED

STATS

Age	27
Born	10 August 1971, Cork
Size	5'11", 12st 1lbs
Position	Midfielder

Club	**League Apps**	**League Goals**
Nottingham Forest	114	22
Manchester United	156	19

Irish International

42 appearances, 5 goals

Transfers

Cobh Ramblers to Forest, June 1990, £10,000
Forest to Man Utd, July 1993, £3.75m

Honours

European Cup 1999; Premiership 1994, 1996, 1997, 1999; FA Cup 1994, 1996, 1999, Runner-up 1991 (Forest); League Cup Runner-up 1992 (Forest)

Memorable United Match

With United 2-0 down to Juventus early in this season's Champions League Semi-Final, they were desperate for a goal. It was Roy whose header on a corner gave United hope, and they went on to win 3-2 and reach the final.

DID YOU KNOW

Roy's United debut was at Wembley – in the 1993 Charity Shield against Arsenal.

WHO NEEDS Eric Cantona? Alex Ferguson reckons he has the perfect replacement for the mercurial Frenchman as his general on the field.

Roy Keane has that same spark of red devilment about him and has grown into the natural leader of a young United side that has achieved so much and seems sure to win even more before the combative 27-year-old Irishman retires.

Keane's fiery temperament – he is a former amateur boxer – often leads him to clash with officials, but Fergie and Irish manager Mick McCarthy are adamant when they plead with Keane: 'Don't you ever change!'

Yet Keane has calmed down a great deal, by his old tinderbox standards. No-one could ever doubt the commitment which has earned Keane a place among Europe's top midfielders. 'Above all else Roy's a competitor,' says the United boss. 'When the ball's there to be won, he doesn't hold back. That's what makes him into the player he is. As a captain, he sets down the benchmarks for the rest. And he's done the job brilliantly.

'Eric Cantona was a hard act to follow as team captain. But in a different way, Roy is proving just as good. He is my new Cantona.'

McCarthy handed Keane the Republic of Ireland captain's armband when Andy Townsend quit international football – barely a year after Keane refused to join a summer tour of America in 1996.

'Despite some of the things that were said in the papers, I never had any problem with Roy on or off the pitch,' says McCarthy. 'When Andy packed it in, there was never any doubt in my mind who should succeed him.

Keane is dedicated to winning every ball

'Apart from his other qualities, Roy has a real presence on the pitch and that's a very important aspect of the job.

Captaincy for club and country has made Keane a better player, says McCarthy. 'He's as dedicated as ever to winning every tackle. But these days he doesn't allow himself to get involved in scrapes in other areas of the pitch. Instead he's reading the game for others. And that's a tremendous help to the younger players in the side.'

Little wonder that Keane, is now United's best-paid player after attempts to lure him abroad for £20m.

HARRY KEWELL

LEEDS UNITED

STATS

Age	20
Born	22 September 1978, Sydney, Australia
Size	5'11", 12st 0lbs
Position	Midfielder

Club	League Apps	League Goals
Leeds United	70	11

Australian International

Transfers

None, signed from New South Wales Academy

Honours

None

Memorable United Match

Harry played a vital part in one of the best Leeds performances of 1998-99, setting up Jimmy Floyd Hasselbaink for the home side's goal in their 1-1 draw with Manchester United in late April. He waltzed through the red defence before setting up the Dutchman.

DID YOU KNOW

Harry may play for Australia, but says he 'used to pretend that I was Paul Gascoigne when I was a kid'! Now he plays against Gascoigne, of course – and does rather better.

AT THE latest count there were getting on for 50 Aussies in British soccer.

And none, apart from Man United's Mark Bosnich, has made a bigger impact here than 20-year-old Harry Kewell, Leeds' midfield maestro – one very much in the Johnny Giles mould.

Aussie Test twins Mark and Steve Waugh trod a similar early path to Kewell – and England's bowlers have since wished that the pair had gone for the white of Leeds rather than the whites and baggy green cap in which they have since become feared.

'I was a bit of a backyard all-rounder,' recalls Kewell. But football won him over the day he first saw English footy on television back in his native Sydney.

Leeds, naturally, are thrilled that Kewell found it easy to turn his back on cricket. They paid the princely sum of £2,400 for a player now rated in the £5m class. He has been pulling the strings for resurgent Leeds, making them one of the brightest and most entertaining teams in the country. And never has Harry boy been homesick.

But Leeds have re-thought their policy on spreading the net for young talent Down Under. With Kewell's call-ups for his country often keeping him out of his club side at vital times in the Premiership season, Leeds are now insisting that all new Aussie recruits – and there are more on the way – must be qualified to play for England and renounce their claims to play for Australia.

That is not an option for Kewell. He dons the gold and green with pride – and it still hurts to recall how close he was to appearing on the big World Cup stage in France a year ago.

He'd scored in the play-off first leg against Iran, silencing a hostile 100,000-strong Tehran crowd. And he notched again as the Terry Venables-coached Aussies went 2-0 up only to heartbreakingly concede two late strikes and go out on away goals.

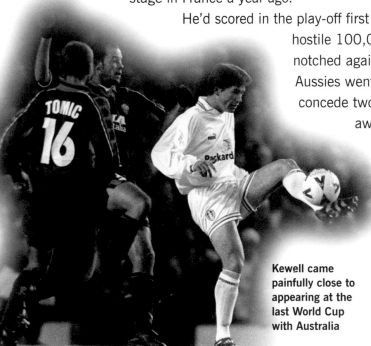

Kewell came painfully close to appearing at the last World Cup with Australia

He aims to make up for his disappointment at the 2000 Olympics in Sydney.

'It's on home turf and I'd love to be able to retire with an Olympic gold medal in my collection,' he says.

Few would bet, at his current rate of progress, that it would be the only major reward coming his way...

FRANK LAMPARD

WEST HAM UNITED

STATS

Age	21
Born	20 June 1978, Romford
Size	6'0", 11st 12lbs
Position	Midfielder

Club	League Apps	League Goals
West Ham	84	9
Swansea (loan)	9	1

England

No full international appearances

Transfers

None, signed from trainee

Honours

None

Memorable Hammers' Match

In the 1997-98 season, Frank put on a superb display in the Worthington Cup against Walsall. He scored one early goal to give the Hammers a 1-0 lead, but then scored two second half goals in just over a minute to seal his hat trick, and a 4-1 win.

DID YOU KNOW

Frank's dad didn't score many goals for West Ham, but he did get one of the most famous in their history – the one that beat Everton to take the Hammers to the 1980 FA Cup Final.

Like father, like son... Frank is carrying on the family tradition at Upton Park

FRANK LAMPARD would appear to have the football world at his feet – at just 21 he's an England skipper, a mainstay of the West Ham side with a queue of suitors keen to tempt him away, and, if you can believe the newspapers, he's dating beautiful TV sports hostess Gabby Yorath.

Tottenham had a £4m transfer bid rejected for the England Under-21 captain, disappointing long-time admirer George Graham, and both Liverpool and Aston Villa are said to be tempted by Lampard's growing reputation in the game.

But he's going nowhere, he says, to delight the Upton Park faithful who have been won over by the mature performances of one of a growing band of Hammers starlets in manager Harry Redknapp's squad.

Lampard could yet scale heights never reached by his famous long-serving Hammer dad, Frank senior, now the London club's assistant manager.

He is that rare item, a midfielder who can get forward and score goals at regular intervals. All successful teams need them, and Lampard's all-round game, allied to his strike rate, was an important factor in the Hammers' solid Premiership show last term and he could well be a Hammer skipper of the future.

Redknapp is desperate to keep his home-grown stars, tempted though he may be to cash in on the likes of Lampard, Rio Ferdinand and even Joe Cole. The Hammers boss says: 'Frank is the future of the club, and it is vital that we keep him at Upton Park. He has made excellent progress and has committed himself to a long-term deal with the club, which shows just the sort of commitment I want to see from my young players.'

Having a famous dad at the club makes it harder in many ways, though Lampard junior says: 'I suppose there is more pressure on you, as people will always say you're being given special treatment.

'But the reverse is usually true. In any case it doesn't worry me.'

The Romford-born youngster signed pro forms with West Ham in 1995 and has risen through the ranks steadily with club and country ever since. Glenn Hoddle had him earmarked for a fast-track route into the senior England side before his resignation, but Lampard's continuing development is sure to give him his big chance under Kevin Keegan.

HENRIK LARSSON

CELTIC

STATS

Age	27
Born	29 September 1971, Helsingborg, Sweden
Size	5'10", 11st 11lbs
Position	Striker

Club	League Apps	League Goals
Celtic	70	44

Swedish International

Transfers Involving British Clubs

Feyenoord to Celtic, July 1997, £650,000

Honours

Scottish League 1998; Scottish Cup Runner-Up 1999;

Memorable Celtic Match

Celtic needed to win their last match of the 1997-98 season to be sure of the championship for the first time in ten years. Henrik took just three minutes to put his team on the way to glory, breaking in from the left and shooting home from 20 yards. It settled the team's nerves and they ran out 2-0 winners.

DID YOU KNOW

Henrik was voted Sweden's Footballer Of The Year in 1998

WITH HIS flowing dreadlocks, it is not easy to mistake Scotland's highest-paid footballer, the Swedish striker Henrik Larsson.

He has just signed a new £2m-a-year deal with Celtic and was voted Player of the Year in Scotland, making him a household name.

It was something of a surprise, then, when someone not blessed with the same looks and hairstyle went on a £1,900 spree with the player's stolen credit card earlier this year. The man used the card 25 times to buy designer clothes, jewellery and a range of CDs. He even bought pet food from a supermarket!

Larsson shrugged it off – with an £8m deal in his pocket he could afford to – and the man was later jailed. And such matters won't put Larsson off his elegant and effective stride.

He now has Kenny Dalglish as his boss, but Larsson used to idolise Kevin Keegan – and even has one of his football shirts. Scotland's newly-crowned double Player of the Year collected his prized souvenir when Celtic played Newcastle in a testimonial match. He used to watch Liverpool on TV at home in Sweden and became a big fan when Keegan was wowing the Kop.

Dalglish, of course, followed in Keegan's footsteps at Liverpool and then as Newcastle boss. And Larsson is the biggest Celtic icon since Dalglish left Parkhead for Anfield in 1977. He loves the former Scottish champions, who lost their coveted crown to Old Firm rivals Rangers last term, and is committed to turning the tide back towards the green and white half of Glasgow.

'I played in the World Cup Finals for Sweden and that was a dream come true. I played in the semi-finals of a European competition when Feyenoord lost to Rapid Vienna. Going a long way in Europe with Celtic is one of the ambitions I hope to achieve during the next four years,' he says.

There was no-one even near Larsson in the race to be Scotland's best player last season. 'It certainly made me very proud and justified my decision to stay in Scotland.'

His partnership with Mark Viduka was one of the most lethal in the game and many believe they could go on to rival Ally McCoist and Mark Hateley as one of the all-time great strike pairings in the Scottish game.

Larsson has easily outwitted many opponents in the Scottish Premier League

NIGEL MARTYN

LEEDS UNITED

A NIGGLING KNEE INJURY that needed close-season surgery upset Nigel Martyn's plans to take over from David Seaman as England's No. 1.

Martyn, now 32 and committed to Leeds United for the rest of his career, doesn't believe that the Arsenal keeper is losing his edge. But he knows he needs to be at the top of his form in order to have a chance of being at the top of coach Kevin Keegan's list.

'I heard some suggestions that David was not having the best of times for club or country and that he was under pressure,' says Martyn.

'There was a bit of a whispering campaign going on, saying that he was letting his standards slip and maybe wasn't up to being the England keeper any more. But you will never hear a word of that from me or any of the other keepers in the England squad. As far as we're concerned he's still the main man.

'You only have to look at him in training. He is a giant and he is still the best we have in this country – but I wouldn't be honest if I said I didn't want his place in the side.'

Martyn has ambitions to be England's number one

Martyn, immaculate as ever as Leeds stormed to fourth in the Premiership last term, says he knows the clock is ticking. 'I'm incredibly ambitious and I want to be the England No.1.'

He wants to play for his country in a major championship and fears that the next World Cup might come too late for him – he'll be 35 – having been in Glenn Hoddle's squad last time.

He has been a clean sheet specialist, with Leeds conceding only nine goals at home last term, and says he owes George Graham, David O'Leary's predecessor, for overall improvements to his game.

The giant Cornishman is a superb shot-stopper but has learned to use his physical presence to impose himself on his penalty area.

'George pointed us in the right direction and David's appointment has meant continuity. As a club, we feel we can build on last season when we had a change of management but still finished well in the table.

'I think there are exciting times ahead, especially with so many talented youngsters coming through at Elland Road, and the pattern well established here now,' he says.

GARY NEVILLE
MANCHESTER UNITED

DID YOU KNOW

Gary and Phil have another England international in the family – their sister, Tracey. But her talents lie in netball, rather than football.

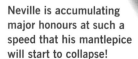

Neville is accumulating major honours at such a speed that his mantlepiece will start to collapse!

GARY NEVILLE is Mr Cool as he arrives for training at United's Cliff ground in Salford. But, while his team-mates roll up in flash Ferraris, the England defender rolls up on his push-bike! Not that he can't afford a decent set of wheels. Indeed, he is the proud owner of a £40,000 Mercedes.

It's just that Neville is not one to flaunt his wealth and is just as happy to pedal to work, like many of his admiring fans, on a mountain bike – and wearing his football boots!

On the pitch, Neville's boots have done the talking again. He was one of five United stars named in the season's top Premiership XI, along with David Beckham, Dennis Irwin, Jaap Stam and Dwight Yorke.

That, and even more silverware for the family trophy cabinet after an epic season at home and in Europe, have firmly franked Neville's place in Old Trafford history and made him a first choice for his country.

He had played fewer games for his club (just 19) than any England debutant since World War Two when he made his bow against Japan in 1995. He has now played more than 30 times for his country, including some outstanding performances in the World Cup in France.

But, while many continue to sing the 23-year-old Bury-born defender's praises, Neville himself has a real problem with singing. When he lines up for internationals, he refuses to belt out the national anthem. 'I don't feel that singing before a game is part of my normal build-up,' he says.

'A manager can't make you feel proud, just as singing the anthem can't make you play better. I just prefer to try and focus on the game in my own way.'

Neville prefers instead to concentrate on the challenge ahead and produce his usual performance marked by his air of calm authority.

He recognises those qualities in others, notably referees, of whom he was unusually outspoken last season after a series of inconsistent decisions that went against United.

Neville says: 'You just want the referee to keep as low a profile as possible. But sometimes they book and send off players for things like mistimed tackles. If you are asking players not to tackle in a contest of major importance it's not going to happen,' he adds.

'Maybe it is a problem that stems from the top because I know referees are also under a lot of pressure.'

At the same time, he is never one to make excuses for bad results and performances – it merely steels his resolve to do better next time, to become a better player. And, in his position, there are few better these days than Gary Neville.

MARC OVERMARS
ARSENAL

HE'S NEVER simply over the moon – he's Overmars! Arsenal's flying Dutchman is at the height of his powers, despite being viewed as a massive gamble when he joined from Ajax in 1997. Many wondered whether Overmars would ever fully recover from a horrendous knee injury he suffered on a freezing December night at Amsterdam's Olympic Stadium.

He snapped his knee ligaments – a bad enough blow in itself. But when your name is founded on your blistering pace and you miss nine months including Euro 96, there must be a huge question mark on a your ability to recapture previous performance levels.

Paul Gascoigne was never the same player after his knee injury. But Overmars was 22 and says: 'Football wasn't my life, it was my hobby. I didn't worry that it might be over.'

He even suggests be might have become a better player as a result of it. 'I didn't lose any speed.'

It was another injury – this time to his hamstring – that Arsene Wenger believes cost Holland the World Cup in 1998. Overmars missed the semi-final with Brazil after being as instrumental as Arsenal team-mate Dennis Bergkamp in the Dutch side's successful run to the last four.

The words 'Overmars' and pace are synonymous, it seems, though he concedes that Nicolas Anelka may be quicker than him. 'Well, over longer distances. I have a slight edge for the shorter bursts.'

Either way, that raw speed has been a potent weapon in Wenger's Arsenal. The Gunners first showed an interest in Overmars when George Graham was in charge and they monitored the player's fitness battle at Ajax. 'That helped me,' he says. 'I told them I wanted to get fit, and then we'd see about a move.'

Italy was never an option – he finds Serie A football too boring, and says the Premiership can hold its own with any league in Europe.

And Europe is still there to be conquered – the Gunners' Champions' League disappointments last season have merely fired ambitions at Arsenal, he says.

Overmars, of course, knows all about scaling the peaks – he won the Champions' Cup with Ajax in 1995, as well as the World Club Cup. 'It will be very difficult to be the best in Europe, with so many fixtures. But it will not stop us wanting to try,' he says.

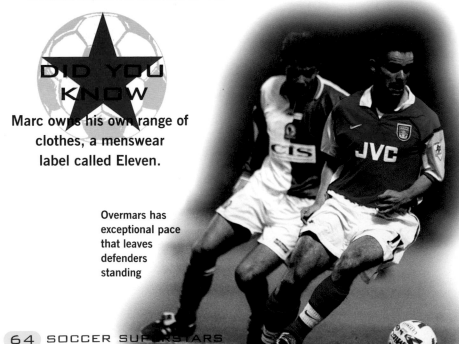

DID YOU KNOW

Marc owns his own range of clothes, a menswear label called Eleven.

Overmars has exceptional pace that leaves defenders standing

MICHAEL OWEN
LIVERPOOL

STATS

Age	19
Born	14 December 1979 Chester
Size	5'8", 11st 0lbs
Position	Striker

Club	League Apps	League Goals
Liverpool	68	37

England International

13 appearances, 4 goals

Transfers

None – signed as trainee

Honours

Carling Player Of The Year 1997-98; BBC Sports Personality Of The Year 1998; Premiership Golden Boot 1997-98 and 1998-99 (both shared); World Cup FIFA Squad Of The Tournament, 1998.

Memorable Liverpool Match

Celtic 2 Liverpool 2, September 1997. Scored on his debut in a defeat at Wimbledon, but a superbly assured goal on his European debut versus Celtic, live on BBC television, demonstrated his enormous talent with an extraordinary maturity for a 17-year-old. Played through at 0-0 after just six minutes in front of a crowd of 48,000 mostly hostile fans, ran 30 yards and calmly beat the keeper.

DID YOU KNOW

In 1998 Michael Owen was the youngest winner of the BBC Sports Personality Of The Year Award, and broke Jimmy Greaves' record as the youngest player to top score in the top flight since World War II.

MICHAEL OWEN is blessed with many things. But instant recall is not one of them. Yet who can blame him when so much has happened to the Liverpool and England striker at such a tender age.

Not yet 20, Owen is the youngest player to be capped for his country this century, he has already reached heights that astonish Reds' legends Ian Rush and Robbie Fowler, and of course is known the world over for one of the greatest goals in World Cup history.

Argentina revels in 'Batigol' – Gabriel Batistuta – but even England's fiercest foes saluted Owen's solo wonder strike that lit up France 98, affectionately christening Owen 'Babygol'.

He is even a brand name now, with mega-deals and commercial packaging putting him on a par with Ronaldo and Eric Cantona. A major American agency bought out his contract with a view to making young Owen a name known in every corner of the world.

His future may yet lay in Italy or on some other foreign field, as daft-money offers keep the Anfield fax machine at full tilt. But Owen is content for the moment at least to wear the Red of Liverpool with pride. He's more Liver Bird than Golden Goose, and the Chester-born youngster's unbridled joy at playing for the Merseyside giants has been evident ever since Roy Evans handed him his Liverpool debut at 17.

'He even had the faith to let me take penalties,' recalls Owen of Gerard Houllier's predecessor and former co-manager. 'He put a lot of trust in me and I'll always respect him for that.'

Evans was always protective of Owen, recognising the boy's special talents, and the game may have much to thank him for in that respect – especially when you see the toll exacted on Ronaldo in recent years.

Defenders have tried all manner of means to shackle Owen. But his sheer, blinding pace is a weapon very few can deal with. 'I get a lot of blocking and shirt-pulling,' he says. 'But then it's up to me to find new ways of hurting them.'

That is just the attitude that seems sure to mark down Owen as one of the English game's legendary figures before he is very much older.

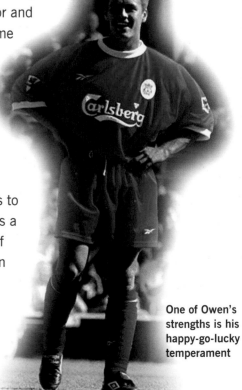

One of Owen's strengths is his happy-go-lucky temperament

EMMANUEL PETIT

ARSENAL

STATS

Age	28	
Born	22 September 1970, Dieppe, France	
Size	6'1", 12st 7lbs	
Position	Midfielder	

Club	League Apps	League Goals
Monaco	222	4
Arsenal	59	6

French International

Transfers

Monaco to Arsenal, July 1997, £3.5m

Honours

World Cup 1998; Premiership 1998; FA Cup 1998; Cup-Winners' Cup Runner-up 1992; French Cup 1991, Runner-up 1989; French Championship 1997

Memorable Gunners' Match

As April 1998 came to a close, the Gunners had to win every game to hang on to their advantage in the championship. Derby came to Highbury, and played well, but they couldn't stop Manu's 30 yard drive that won the match 1-0 and brought the Premiership that much closer for Arsene Wenger's side.

DID YOU KNOW

Holidaying back in Monaco after winning the World Cup, 1998 continued to be Manu's lucky year. He won thousands of pounds in a big-money jackpot, this time from a fruit machine in one of Monte Carlo's famous casinos.

IT WAS a sad sight, a bootless Manu Petit walking crestfallen from the pitch as Arsenal realised their season was over and finishing empty-handed. It was a far cry from ten or so months earlier for Petit.

Then, he had collected Premiership and FA Cup-winner's medals and scored a decisive third goal in the World Cup final.

Perhaps you can't have it all. And last season was always going to be difficult for Petit after what had gone on before. He began the new campaign late, after being allowed to recover from France's World Cup success, and it took him some time to find his elegant stride again. His frustrations at grappling for his best form led him to red cards and stories of a quick exit from the Premiership, back to France. But Arsene Wenger, the Gunner's boss, was able to talk to his on-field general in his own tongue and on his own terms, and gradually enticed Petit back towards his best form.

Petit has been a revelation since his unheralded £3.5m move to Arsenal from AS Monaco. But he says: 'Winning the Double in my first season was unbelievable and was always going to be tough to follow.'

Petit was France's Young Player of the Year in 1990. But, at 18, losing his brother, who died while playing football, almost caused him to throw in the towel. And he felt like quitting Highbury after only three games. He says: 'I'd always wanted to play in England and thought that physically and mentally I was ready, but I wasn't prepared for the fight and power on the pitch.

Petit feels he is sometimes unfairly targeted by refs

'After my third game, against Southampton, I told my fiancee that I didn't think I could be fit for the next game.

'I could have gone back to France inside two weeks but I knew it would have been a big mistake. But I'm not a loser. So I told myself I had to stay and give my best.'

Petit is a laid-back character – he has been labelled 'The Unpassionate Man'. He shies away from the attention that star-status brings, but enjoys the finer things in life – good wine, going to the theatre or for dinner in smart restaurants. He also likes letting his hair down with his team-mates.

Refreshed and renewed after a less stressful summer, and fired by last season's disappointment, you can bet on Petit and Co. bouncing back with a vengeance.

KEVIN PHILLIPS
SUNDERLAND

STATS

Age	26	
Born	25 July 1973, Hitchin	
Size	5'7", 11st 0lbs	
Position	Striker	

Club	League Apps	League Goals
Watford	59	24
Sunderland	71	54

England International

1 appearance, no goals

Transfers

Baldock Town to Watford, December 1994, £10,000

Watford to Sunderland, July 1997, £600,000

Honours

Division One 1999

Memorable Mackems' Match

With a 5-2 win at Bury in April 1999, Sunderland achieved promotion back to the Premiership, thanks in large part on the night to no fewer than four goals from Kevin.

DID YOU KNOW

Kevin's chance to move from midfield to striker with Baldock only came with a phone call from the manager, ringing to see if he felt up to the switch to help out in an injury crisis.

Phillips capped a superb season with an international call-up

FOR ANY Park footballer, the story of Kevin Phillips is proof that fairytales can come true. A few year ago, the Sunderland goal king was cleaning Alan Shearer's boots. Little could he know that he'd make his England debut alongside the man he idolised since their days at Southampton.

Shearer, of course, moved on apace. Phillips fell by the wayside, later stacking shelves in a Dixons warehouse and playing his football part-time for non-League Baldock Town in front of a barely a couple of hundred fans. Now he performs in front of full houses at newly-promoted Sunderland and is rated in the £7m class after three years as a proven goalscorer.

He might have been a shock inclusion for the friendly against Hungary, but Kevin Keegan had been impressed by his pace, mobility and eye for goal. The 26-year-old was surprised by his call-up: 'I thought I'd never get a chance. Niall Quinn had put my name forward for Ireland, and I think Wales were also seeing if I qualified to play for them,' he said.

At Baldock he switched from midfield to up front – and there was no stopping him. Watford took a chance and, three years later, Sunderland paid £600,000 for him. He's struck almost 60 goals in 80 starts for Peter Reid's side and now revels in his chance to do it at the highest level.

'When I first got the England call, I thought Peter Reid was having me on. It's been a fairytale for me. Especially after the injury troubles I've had. I missed a year at Watford with an injury and thought I'd never play again. Then, last season, I had similar doubts again when I had four months on the sidelines.

Former Southampton boss Chris Nicholl, who used the apprentice Phillips at right back, released him from the Dell. Phillips never forgot and recalls: 'I always said that I would prove him wrong, and I think I've done that.'

Things got better and better for Phillips last term as Sunderland returned to the Premiership after their play-off heartache 12 months earlier against Charlton. A wonder goal by Phillips sparked the champagne celebration as Sunderland finally clinched the First Division title at Barnsley.

Sunderland fans love him – and he's staying there, despite interest from Arsenal and West Ham. 'I am loving my time at Sunderland and I would be daft to even think of leaving,' he says. 'I signed a four-year deal last year and I am happy to complete that.'

NIALL QUINN

SUNDERLAND

Age	32
Born	6 October 1966, Dublin, Ireland
Size	6'4", 12st 4lbs
Position	Striker

Club	League Apps	League Goals
Arsenal	67	14
Manchester City	203	66
Sunderland	88	36

Irish International

68 appearances, 17 goals

Transfers

Arsenal to Man City, March 1990, £800,000

Man City to Sunderland, August 1996, £1.3m

Honours

League Cup 1987 (Arsenal); Division One Championship 1999

Memorable Mackems' Match

Niall has played many memorable games, but in April 1999 he scored the goal that put Peter Reid's side 2-1 up at Bury as they won 5-2 to seal the Division One Championship.

NIALL QUINN put his previous play-off heartbreak behind him when Sunderland won the First Division championship last season at a canter.

And this thoroughbred striker not only played a major part in the success, but he showed his big-heartedness along the way, netting £2,500 for the homeless of Sunderland with a £40 charity bet on Grand National winner Bobbyjo. That sort of spirit showed that the Wearsiders were not going to fall at the final fence again.

Quinn had scored twice as they suffered a shocking play-off defeat against Charlton at Wembley 12 months earlier. Typically, the genial giant Irishman was one of the first of Sunderland's devastated squad to shrug off the disappointment and vow that the side would bounce back even stronger.

They did so in emphatic style, with Quinn in harness with livewire Kevin Phillips. It was a £1.3m switch to Sunderland in 1996 that revitalised Quinn's ailing career at a struggling Manchester City. He scored the first ever goal at Sunderland's new Stadium of Light, ironically in a 3-1 victory over his former club, City.

The 32-year-old has pledged the rest of his career to Sunderland by agreeing a new three-year deal, after Leeds boss David O'Leary expressed an interest in him.

He scored his 100th League goal last term in more than 300 games and is enjoying an Indian summer to a career he feared would be ended through persistent knee injury two year ago. 'The bones had fused in my legs and I couldn't bend or straighten them. I couldn't jump properly.

'It wouldn't get better until I had the last of six operations. I had even talked about taking my pension.'

When he does eventually quit, he'll probably do something with horses. 'I love to breed them and I get tremendous satisfaction caring for sick horses.'

He stables five horses around his two-acre woodland home, and nursing ailing horses back to fitness strikes a chord with him after his own injury problems.

One of his star turns could be aptly-named Premier Project. It has been struggling for fitness for two years having earlier won some decent races on the Flat.

Quinn has pledged to end his fabulous career with Sunderland

DID YOU KNOW

This will be the second time Niall has played under Peter Reid for Sunderland in the top flight – and Reid was also Niall's boss at Manchester City when they finished fifth in the old First Division in 1991.

DAVID SEAMAN
ARSENAL

ENGLAND'S NO 1 is as secure as he as ever been in the position, despite his advancing years and recurrent injury problems. The Arsenal keeper clocked up his 50th cap last spring, in the 1-1 draw in Hungary – a night on which he pulled off a string of superb saves and was beaten only by a wickedly curling free-kick. It's unwise to mention that it was not dissimilar to the famous Paul Gascoigne effort that left him stranded at Wembley in the 1991 FA Cup semi-final...

Seaman clearly didn't bear Gazza any grudges, for the chirpy Geordie stole the show at his celebrity wedding reception at fairytale Castle Ashby, with a solo turn on the drums.

Besides his wedding to Debbie Rodgers, last season was the usual mixed bag for England's Euro96 hero and World Cup stalwart. Seaman was in immaculate form for the Gunners, despite the ever-present threat of young Austrian starlet Alex Manninger. There was even talk last summer of Juventus making a record £5m bid for Seaman, but the man signed from QPR for £1.3m more than eight years ago, was never going to leave Highbury.

In December he suffered a shoulder injury against Aston Villa and feared his season would be over. Manninger stepped in – then injured his wrist saving a shot in training from Seaman, missing the rest of the season!

Seaman has now played almost 450 games for the Gunners, making him a living Highbury legend, and won two championships and two FA Cups as well as the League Cup and Cup-Winners' Cup. Provided he stays fit and maintains his form (even he couldn't be blamed for Ryan Giggs' epic, solo Cup semi-final replay winner), Seaman could stay an Arsenal regular for at least another two years.

When he does decide to hang up his gloves, he may try TV. He's already made an appearance in Brookside, playing himself, opening a club in the Channel 4 soap.

Seaman has long been a key part of Arsenal's superb defence

'I watch the programme all the time. I don't know about a future in acting and I'm not planning on packing up yet.' Seaman gets his kicks from coaching a local pub side – and has turned Chiltern FC, based at the Blue Ball in Ashridge, from no-hopers to double winners. A year on from Arsenal's wonderful Premiership and Cup double, it was the only silverware for Seaman last season!

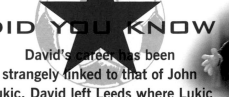

DID YOU KNOW

David's career has been strangely linked to that of John Lukic. David left Leeds where Lukic was establishing himself, but then replaced him at Arsenal in 1990, Lukic going back to Leeds. Then in 1996 Lukic came back to Highbury, to be David's reserve.

ALAN SHEARER
NEWCASTLE UNITED

STATS

Age	28	
Born	13 October 1970, Newcastle	
Size	6'0", 12st 6lbs	
Position	Striker	

Club	League Apps	League Goals
Southampton	118	23
Blackburn Rovers	138	112
Newcastle United	77	41

England International

50 appearances, 23 goals

Transfers

Southampton to Blackburn, July 1992 £3.6m
Blackburn to Newcastle, July 1996 £15m

Honours

Premiership 1995; FA Cup runner-up 1998, 1999; PFA Player Of The Year 1995, 1997; Football Writers' Player Of The Year 1994; Premiership Top Scorer 1995, 1996, 1997; Tournament Top Scorer, Euro 96.

Memorable Magpies' Match

With Newcastle 3-1 down at home to Leicester on 2 February 1997, goals in the 77th, 83rd and 90th minutes gave Shearer his first hat-trick for the club, landing a hugely improbable 4-3 win.

DID YOU KNOW

Shearer was signed for Newcastle by Kevin Keegan. 14 years earlier, when KK had been a playing hero on Tyneside rather than the manager, the young Shearer was pictured in the local paper meeting his hero.

IF ALAN SHEARER was a company, his share price would have fallen dramatically in the last year.

From England captain, leading a side he claimed was one of the best in the world into the World Cup finals in France, and FA Cup final skipper, Shearer's stock has been in decline. There have even been calls in certain quarters to drop the £15m Newcastle United striker from the England side.

The argument goes that Shearer has not been the same player since his near year-long injury lay-off following a broken ankle and extensive ligament damage, and that he is not a natural partner for Michael Owen. A year ago, the prospect of a Shearer-less England would have been unthinkable.

So has injury taken the edge off the Shearer that prompted Newcastle to break the bank, and put fear into foreign defences?

Well, he has never been known for his pace and can't dribble past players, but you write off Alan Shearer at your peril. As former England boss Glenn Hoddle says: 'Alan has magnificent mental strength. He works so hard for his team-mates and is not afraid to put himself about physically. He is a clever player who can understand tactics, even if it means having to defend.'

That was never more apparent than in England's brave World Cup defeat by Argentina. Shearer played deep on the right flank after David Beckham was sent off, and produced a disciplined performance, with Owen ploughing away on his own up front.

Shearer is out to prove that he is still the best striker in the game

Shearer's goal record is a target to be shot at – he was the first to score 100 goals in the Premiership, and to bag more than 30 goals in three successive seasons. We might now be seeing a new-look Shearer emerging – one that could prove as dangerous as ever, if not more so.

Players – especially strikers – often appear to lose their way. With Newcastle having twice undergone transformations in recent years, Shearer has probably not been used to his fullest potential. But there were signs towards the end of last term, as the Magpies reached a second successive Cup Final, that Shearer was about to leave the critics choking on their words.

ALAN SMITH
LEEDS UNITED

FORMER LEEDS and Manchester United winger Lee Sharpe reckons Alan Smith and the rest of the Elland Road boys wonders can become the Old Trafford club's biggest rivals in the years ahead – and even overtake them.

Sharpe, who was sold by Leeds to First Division runners-up Bradford City this summer, grew up with the Manchester youth graduates David Beckham, Paul Scholes, Nicky Butt and Phil and Gary Neville.

But he says: 'These Leeds kids are every bit as good as Becks and Co were at the same age. And they are only going to get better.'

King among them is Smith, the striker who didn't figure in many reference books last season – but soon made a name for himself with his precocious finishing and coolness.

'Alan Smith is incredible,' says Sharpe. 'Talk about an old head on young shoulders at just 18.

'He has terrific ability, but also possesses an excellent temperament.

Like all the best goalscorers, he is ice-cool and clinical in the penalty area and instinctively knows when it is the right time for him to be selfish.'

Sharpe says Smith has a tremendous awareness about bringing other players into the game – 'and he's a kid you don't mess with, either. He won't let opponents rough him up because he is well capable of showing a little aggressive streak when it is needed'.

Indeed, Smith suffered a couple of suspensions last season – a campaign that didn't begin for him until November when he scored at Anfield with his first touch in Premiership football.

Leeds boss David O'Leary rates him very highly indeed and says: 'He is a special talent and I have no doubt that he will go on to play for England.'

In doing so, he would emulate former Leeds great Allan Clarke, with whom many have drawn comparisons. Leeds chairman Peter Ridsdale is one. He says: 'Smith has many of Clarkie's qualities, such as that touch of arrogance to go with a supreme confidence in front of goal.

'Clarke knew when to go on his own and when to lay it off. Alan Smith has obviously got the balance right, too. People are going to hear a lot of this young lad for a long time to come.'

DID YOU KNOW

Alan might have helped beat Liverpool by scoring on his debut – but before joining Leeds he used to support the Anfield club.

Smith is just one of the many promising youngsters that give Leeds a bright future

GARETH SOUTHGATE
ASTON VILLA

DID YOU KNOW

Gareth is keen to go into the media when he gives up the game, and took a journalism course for a BBC radio show when he was at Crystal Palace.

IT HAS been a mixed time for Gareth Southgate. Having all but buried the memories of his Euro 96 penalty-miss heartbreak, the Aston Villa skipper has been one of the Premiership's most consistent defenders.

He was a key figure as Villa mounted a serious title challenge last term. Sadly it wilted – and Southgate suffered a major snub as Glenn Hoddle's reign as England coach came to a close.

Southgate, now 28, thought Hoddle would ask him to lead the side for the first time against the Czech Republic last term – but he was overlooked in favour of Tottenham's Sol Campbell. He didn't even make the starting line-up.

Southgate had dashed from wife Alison's hospital bedside following the birth of their first child, daughter Mia. Hoddle clearly felt Southgate might be distracted by it all.

But Villa boss John Gregory fumed: 'Gareth should be captain of England – and will be in my opinion. He is without question the outstanding English defender in the Premiership.

'No-one has come anywhere near his level of performance recently.'

Gregory had earlier been thrilled at Southgate's decision to sign a £6m five-year deal that effectively means he will see out his playing days with the club.

He said: 'I was convinced he would be gone after the World Cup. He came back from France to see Steve Staunton gone, Dwight Yorke was going and maybe Mark Bosnich, too.

'I had to convince Gareth that we had a big future and that wasn't easy.'

Southgate had criticised Villa, publically accusing the club of lack of ambition.

Signed by former boss Brian Little from Crystal Palace for £2.5m four seasons ago, the England man said at the time: 'I felt the club was underachieving and that was also down to the players.'

But he soon came round as Gregory put the smile back on the Villa faces. Southgate apologised for his comments and said: 'I really feel that we can now become one of the best clubs in the business.

'I accepted a long-term deal because I was impressed with the way John Gregory has gone about his job – on and off the pitch. He has shown that Villa can now join the Premiership elite.'

Southgate is recognised as one of the Premiership's best defenders

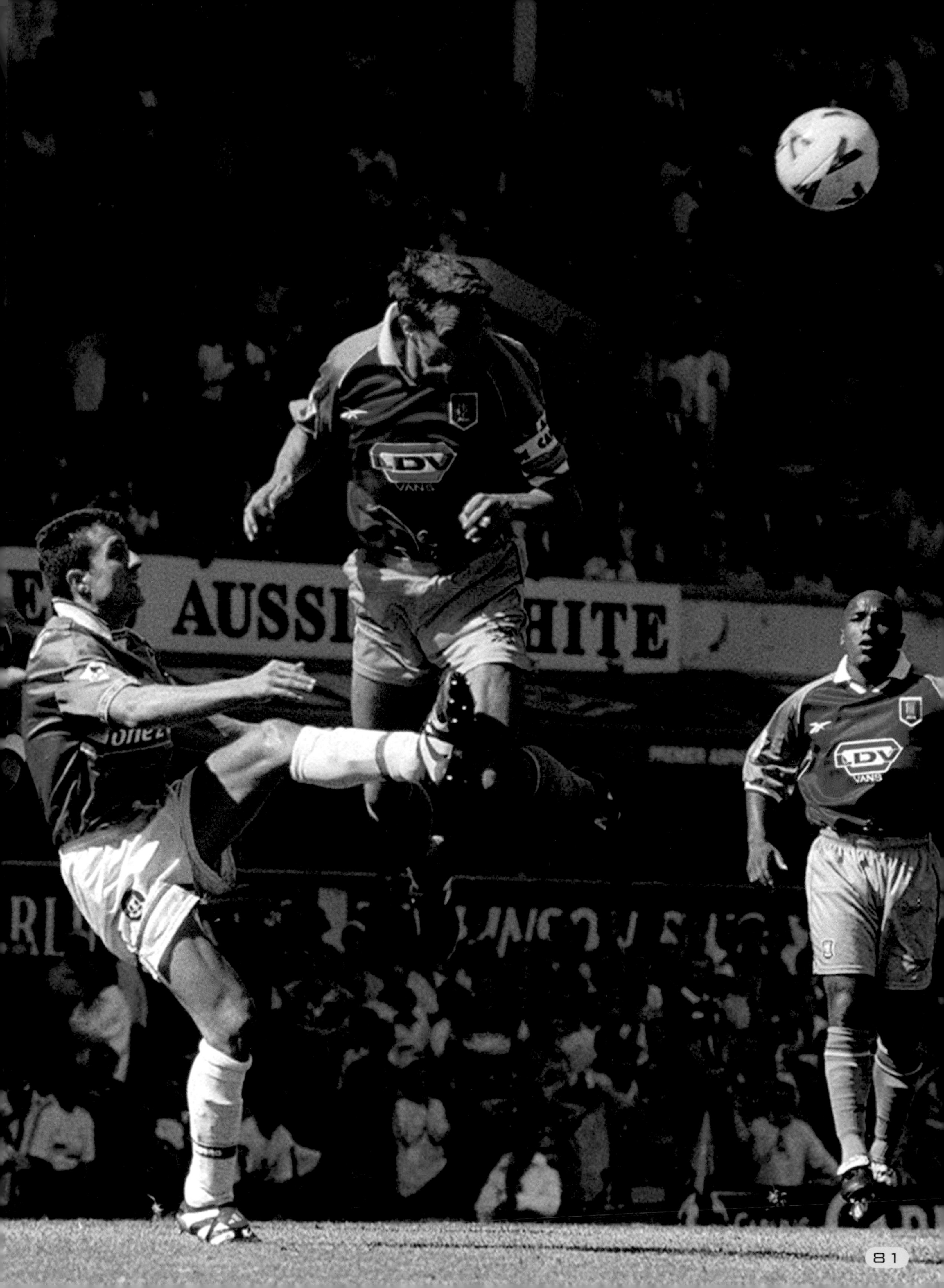
AUSSI
HITE
LDV
VANS

JAAP STAM
MANCHESTER UNITED

STATS

Age	27
Born	17 July 1972, Kampen, Netherlands
Size	6'3", 13st 8lbs
Position	Defender

Club	League Apps	League Goals
Manchester United	30	1

Dutch International

Transfers

PSV to Man Utd, July 1998, £10.75m

Honours

European Cup 1999; Premiership 1999; FA Cup 1999; Dutch League 1997; Dutch Cup Runner-Up 1998; Dutch Footballer Of The Year 1998

Memorable United Match

The European Cup Final in Barcelona capped Jaap's brilliant first year with United, and while it took late goals to bring home the trophy, Jaap helped keep Bayern Munich from extending their lead earlier in the game. It's certainly a match he'll never forget.

DID YOU KNOW

Jaap was so keen to come to Old Trafford he waived his right under his PSV contract to a 15% cut of the transfer fee.

THE DUTCH know a thing or two about putting up solid barriers. After all, when your country lies for the most part the equivalent height of a double-decker bus below sea-level, it becomes a natural priority. It seems apt, then, that the giant dam in what had been a depressingly leaky Manchester United defence should be Dutch.

Yet Jaap Stam's £10.75m arrival from PSV Eindhoven last summer raised many eyebrows. Fans wondered whether this giant Orange would prove to be an expensive lemon. Stam had looked vulnerable to pace in the World Cup, as Holland reached the semi-finals, and there were disparaging comments aplenty when he first pulled on the red of United. 'A tree trunk,' was one of the kindest. But Stam has a heart of oak and quickly proved to be one of Alex Ferguson's shrewdest-ever signings.

While Dwight Yorke plundered opposing defences, David Beckham brilliantly shrugged off his World Cup woes, and Peter Schmeichel decided to hang up his goalkeeping gloves, Stam stood firm. He was ready for Premiership football. When he was with lowly PEC Zwolle, he had a trial with Sheffield Wednesday but thought it too early to try to crack England.

'I was a bit nervous about the transfer fee at first,' admits Stam, who soon overcame his early stutterings to underline the verdict of Johan Cruyff – 'he's the best defender in Europe'.

And he proved it as United beat both Inter Milan and Juventus en route to lift the Treble, including their first European Cup in 31 years.

Holland is known for its bulbs but the flowering talent of Jacobus 'Jaap' Stam once seemed set to handle a different type altogether – he trained as an electrician. 'I'd have been fitting switches and light bulbs if I hadn't gone into football,' he says.

He still has a house in Holland, but his wife Ellis – whom he's known since they were teenagers – and new daughter Lisa are very much at home now in England. The cats are out of quarantine, forever eyeing the goldfish, named Castor Troy after the villain in Stam's favourite movie Face Off, in which John Travolta and Nicholas Cage swap faces.

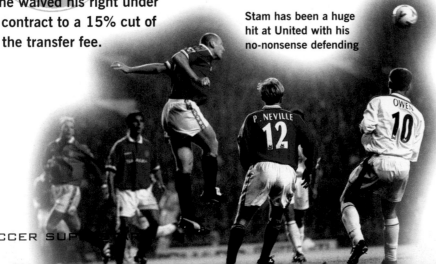

Stam has been a huge hit at United with his no-nonsense defending

Stam never needs to go that far – a simple exchange of glances with the man he's marking is enough to establish his position as the guardian of Old Trafford.

You'll have to go via Holland to get round him. Some tree-trunk!

CHRIS SUTTON
BLACKBURN ROVERS

DID YOU KNOW

In spite of all the players brought to Ewood Park in recent years, Chris was Blackburn's record signing from the summer of 1994 until Kevin Davies was signed in 1998.

CHRIS SUTTON is almost back to his old SAS best after a nightmare year he reckons has been the worst of his career. Spurned by his country and having suffered a string of nagging injuries, the Blackburn Rovers striker, and skipper following Tim Sherwood's departure to Spurs, has been rejuvenated, despite Rovers being relegated.

Sutton's international career was seemingly over before it began following a bust-up with former coach Glenn Hoddle. But their differences were about to be patched up when Hoddle was sacked in February, and Kevin Keegan immediately recalled the Rovers man to the England fold.

Knee ligament damage from a crunching challenge by Aston Villa's Ugo Ehiogu cost Sutton a six-week lay-off just after Christmas that didn't help Rovers' Premiership survival hopes.

He'd already missed much of the earlier part of the season with stress fractures of both feet. And in February, he had a series of scans that finally killed off fears that he might need an operation on his right foot and thus miss the rest of the season.

He said: 'It was grim. A complete and absolute nightmare. I had a bad time a year earlier with injuries, but 1998 was simply unbelievable.

'Knee injuries are a worry but I was very lucky. It could have been a hell of a lot worse. It felt even more frustrating because the team was struggling and I could do nothing much about it.'

What didn't help were persistent stories of Sutton flying the Ewood Park coop.

A Premiership winner back in the days when he and Alan Shearer were the most feared strike pairing in the game, Sutton was linked with rumours of a £10m move to Chelsea. Sutton immediately phoned Rovers' owner Jack Walker to assure him there was no substance to any of the stories. 'I'm happy at Blackburn,' he said.

And Brian Kidd has no doubt about the value of Sutton to Rovers: 'He has a heart as big as a dustbin lid, is a tremendous leader and sets an excellent example which is good for the younger players.'

'He is a quality striker. If I could have any striker in the Premiership, Sutton would always be my first choice.'

Relegation, though, has put Sutton back on many clubs' shopping lists.

Sutton has experienced the highs and lows of life with Blackburn

PATRICK VIEIRA

ARSENAL

DID YOU KNOW

Patrick was up against a familiar face when he made his debut for France in 1997 – Dennis Bergkamp was playing against him for Holland.

Vieira has a World Cup under his belt and now wants to win more trophies at club level

PATRICK VIEIRA will never change his ultra-combative ways. Indeed, while rival clubs' managers may criticise him for his disciplinary problems, they all secretly long for someone like the 23-year-old giant Frenchman in their engine rooms.

For someone who made an unheralded arrival in the Premiership, just ahead of Gunners boss Arsene Wenger, Vieira has won a World Cup – and a permanent place in the hearts of Arsenal fans.

His midfield partnership with Manu Petit is the envy of the Premiership and beyond.

Dutch defender Adick Koot, a team-mate at Vieira's first club, AS Cannes, says: 'It's not easy being a world champion at the age of 22 but when you have a talent like Patrick's, you will come through.

'He has the character of a winner and the French No.6 jersey should be his for the next 10 years.

'I remember his debut for Cannes. He was the best player on the pitch. It was incredible. He was only 17, yet he played like a 30-year-old.

'Patrick played one or two-touch football, winning the ball and giving good, clean passes.'

Senegal-born Vieira was given his first-team chance there by Luis Fernandez, who played in the best French midfield ever along with Michel Platini, Alain Giresse and Jean Tigana in France's 1984 European Championship-winning side. Yet even they never won a World Cup, unlike Vieira.

Fernandez's successor at Cannes, Safet Susic. handed Vieira the captain's armband at the age of 19, prompting a move to AC Milan, where he was never given the time to settle. The San Siro club's loss has been Arsenal's undoubted gain.

Vieira made just two Serie A appearances before Wenger – at the time still serving out his contract in Japan with Grampus 8, made him his first transfer target at Highbury.

He paid £3.5m – then a staggering amount for a 20-year-old. But the Gunners' successes since then show that it has been money very well spent.

Wenger says of his prize guy: 'He's still young and sometimes he is singled out by referees.

'Patrick can handle the pressure. I am convinced of it. But he will not change his style of play. It is what makes him so effective.'

DENNIS WISE

CHELSEA

STATS

Age	32
Born	16 December 1966, Kensington, London
Size	5'6", 10st 11lbs
Position	Midfielder

Club	League Apps	League Goals
Wimbledon	135	27
Chelsea	266	46

England International

12 appearances, 1 goal

Transfers

Wimbledon to Chelsea, July 1990, £1.6m

Honours

European Cup Winners' Cup 1998; FA Cup 1988 (Wimbledon), 1997; League Cup 1998; European Super Cup 1998

Memorable Blues' Match

Dennis has won four trophies with Chelsea now, but played a big hand in landing the biggest. It was his perfect pass that enabled Gianfranco Zola to score the goal that won the Cup-Winners' Cup against Stuttgart in 1998.

DID YOU KNOW

At the end of his final game for Wimbledon, a young boy asked Dennis for an autograph – and he gave him the boots he had worn in the game!

Wise and officials have not always seen eye to eye

ALEX FERGUSON once said that Dennis Wise could start an argument in an empty house. It was an accurate description of the Chelsea captain by the Manchester United boss. Wise leaves no-one in any doubt that he is prepared to lay down and die for his club's cause, though Gianluca Vialli would doubtless prefer him not to suffer the stream of suspensions that interrupt his appearances in the Blues' side.

A few seasons ago, Dennis the Menace was pictured doing a forward roll with the FA Cup as the Blues celebrated a Wembley win. Heaven knows what he would do with the Premiership trophy. And that is the one that Wise says drives him on. 'We've won in Europe. We've won the FA Cup. The League is the one I'm missing for the set and I believe we can do it with this club.'

They came within four points of Manchester United's title last season and he believes that they would have done it if the boss had played more often. 'Luca did well in his first season in charge. But there were times, like our European semi-final with Mallorca, when we could have done with his experience.'

That tie, well the first leg, was infamous for another Wise 'naughty' – his alleged ear-biting incident that earned him a rebuke from UEFA.

Initially let go by Southampton, he joined Wimbledon's 'Crazy Gang', and was an influential figure in both their madcap dressing-room antics against team-mates and managers, as well as in the 1988 Cup Final success for the Dons against Liverpool.

In 1997 he became the first Chelsea skipper to lift the same prize at Wembley and the following year added the Coca-Cola and Cup-winners Cups, fashioning crucial goals in both finals. Ruud Gullit, the former Blues boss, was so taken with Wise's spirit and skills that he was surprised England could overlook the 32-year-old's claims. The last of his 12 full caps came some years ago.

Wise is a real rarity – an Englishman at home in a Chelsea squad awash with foreign faces. He plays the part of the chirpy Cockney but was in fact born in an altogether posher part of London, Kensington.

He's now very much a West End Boy, in the manner of Blues heroes of yesteryear.

IAN WALKER
TOTTENHAM HOTSPUR

IAN WALKER is still haunted by the Gianfranco Zola goal that almost ended England's 1998 World Cup campaign virtually before it began.

He is adamant it was not a mistake on his part – a deflection off Sol Campbell took it beyond his grasp and saw the derision of a nation heaped on his shoulders. One cap, one nightmare.

Yet it is Walker's hardened attitude and fighting talk that has seen him reclaim his place in the Tottenham goal and become almost reborn since the arrival of George Graham at White Hart Lane.

Many had predicted his downfall. Walker just laughs: 'I was able to smile quietly to myself when we got to Wembley. I was smiling, thinking of all those people who'd tried to write me off.'

And, at 27, there seem to be only good times ahead for Walker, whose dad Mike was a pro goalkeeper and later manager at Everton and Norwich.

Walker started his young life at centre-forward. At 10, he donned the gloves for the first time and was hooked. 'Dad was in the army and was always very critical when he watched me', Walker recalls. It was at the Lilleshall School of Excellence, at 14, with Andy Cole as a notable fellow class-mate, that Walker matured as a goalkeeper. Perhaps it was the boarding-school regime, and being away from the pressures of home.

DID YOU KNOW

Ian's wife Suzie is a former model, who now presents TV shows on cable and satellite.

Walker has experienced a boost in his career under the guidance of George Graham at Tottenham

Walker is sure, though, that Graham is breathing new life into his career – and the Scotsman's calls for him to be recognised again by his country have made a big difference. 'Suddenly it is fashionable to like Ian Walker again,' says the keeper.

He has benefited from the tougher, tighter regime at the Lane. There's no turning up late for training, a greater attention to detail and, like the rest of his Spurs team-mates, Walker knows exactly what is expected of him in every situation.

Graham pinpoints where he has to distribute the ball, and has encouraged him to dominate the penalty box, almost acting as a sweeper behind the back four.

All the hard work is proving worthwhile. 'In the past we were nowhere near winning anything. Now we've shown what we can do by winning at Wembley – and I'm hungry for success.'

DWIGHT YORKE
MANCHESTER UNITED

STATS

Age	27
Born	3 November 1971, Tobago, Trininad & Tobago
Size	5'9", 12st 3lbs
Position	Striker

Club	League Apps	League Goals
Aston Villa	231	73
Manchester United	32	18

Trinidad & Tobago International

Transfers

Villa to Man Utd, August 1998, £12m

Honours

European Cup 1999; Premiership 1999; FA Cup 1999; League Cup 1996 (Aston Villa)

Memorable United Match

Dwight scored two great goals on David Beckham crosses in United's home leg of the Champions League quarter-final against Inter Milan, moving them towards their historic triumph.

DID YOU KNOW

Dwight is a great friend of West Indies' cricket captain Brian Lara – the pair went to school together, and then were playing in Birmingham for Villa and Warwickshire respectively

DWIGHT YORKE couldn't fail to put the smile on the face of Old Trafford fans. It never leaves his. While Eric Cantona ruled the roost with Gallic shrugs and arrogant aplomb, laid-back Yorke plays with the freedom of a Caribbean breeze, joy lighting up his every move.

The comparison with Cantona is not incidental – when Yorke arrived at Old Trafford just before the Champions' League deadline last August for a staggering £12m from Aston Villa, the Theatre of Dreams was still awash with souvenirs and memories of the great Frenchman who did much to end United's 26-year league title drought.

'It really struck me,' Yorke recalls. 'Eric's remembered for his football genius and I hope some day that people will think of me like that, too.'

The upright collar was the first Cantona trademark to be 'borrowed' by Yorke. 'I thought it was really cool. I never thought copying him like that would be a thing with some fans.'

His goals and his electric partnership with Andy Cole soon won over the most steadfast of non-believers with a famous Treble their reward.

The partnership was a stroke of luck for Alex Ferguson, who admits he had no idea how good it might become. 'I'd planned to play him alongside Patrick Kluivert,' says Fergie. 'But when the two of them clicked – wow'

They bonded immediately – almost like twins – on and off the field, hitting it off from the start. Cole was welcoming and Yorke has brought out the best of him.

Yorke has always been an exciting talent, but United have taken his game to a new level – one that he first dreamed he could reach when he was back in Tobago, playing football on the beach as a kid. When he was seven, he was knocked down by a car and might have died but for the fact a doctor was passing by. He honed his football skills on the sands – and learned valuable lessons about ball control in the house, especially when he broke the family's black and white telly – their pride and joy.

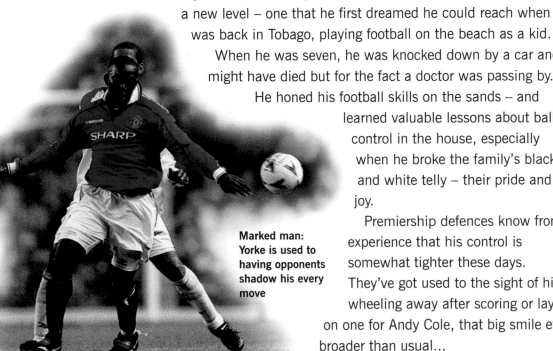

Marked man: Yorke is used to having opponents shadow his every move

Premiership defences know from experience that his control is somewhat tighter these days. They've got used to the sight of him wheeling away after scoring or laying on one for Andy Cole, that big smile even broader than usual...

GIANFRANCO ZOLA

CHELSEA

DID YOU KNOW

Gianfranco famously played for Italy against England in 1997, scoring the goal that beat them at Wembley. But in 1990 he played against them for a local Sardinian side, the Napoli star guesting in a warm-up match before the World Cup.

GIANFRANCO ZOLA can put away spectacular free-kicks in his sleep. But his night-time habits – perhaps reliving those glorious moments – have not made him popular with Chelsea team-mate Roberto di Matteo. 'He snores too much,' says di Matteo. 'I used to share a room with him but I had to throw him out. Now I sleep much better.'

Defenders have to be wide awake to stay with Zola, who reckons his recent form has been even better than when he won the Footballer of the Year award two seasons ago. His manager, Gianluca Vialli says: 'I've spent all my words about him, I don't know what to say now.

'Gianfranco is doing great and not just when we play our offensive football. He has realised in the modern game a striker has to score, but also be the first defender when the opposition has the ball.

'That's not exactly his game but he's working very hard on it and as a manager I'm very pleased. I am also very pleased for him because he's a great guy and cares a lot about the team.'

Stamford Bridge legend Peter Osgood goes even further, saying Zola could be the greatest Chelsea player ever. Osgood helped the Blues to glory in the early 70s. He says: 'Zola had a stunning first season but then had a disappointing year when he was injured a lot and homesick for Italy.

'But he got on with things, got his act together and showed he's a first-class player. He loves to get forward, is a hard worker and has great vision. He also takes players on, which few people can do. He makes goals out of nothing, which marks him out as a special player.'

Zola, now 33, says he wants to finish his career with Chelsea. The sale of Brian Laudrup and long-term injury to Pierluigi Casiraghi, gave him a new lease of life. The absence, too, of Gustavo Poyet, brought added creative demands on Zola – and he didn't disappoint , even if Chelsea did ultimately by finishing a highly promising season without any silverware.

Dedication is Zola's key. He even got the club to build a special £600 'wall' at the club's training ground so that he could practice those stunning free-kicks. They're worth staying awake for...

Zola has proved to be one of the Chelsea fans' all-time favourites